DEVELOPING
SAFETY
TRAINING
PROGRAMS

DEVELOPING SAFETY TRAINING PROGRAMS

Preventing Accidents and Improving Worker Performance through Quality Training

Joseph A. Saccaro

JOHN WILEY & SONS, INC.

New York • Chichester • Weinheim • Brisbane • Singapore • Toronto

Library of Congress Cataloging-in-Publication Data
Saccaro, Joseph A.
    Developing safety training programs / Joseph A. Saccaro.
        p. cm.
    Includes bibliographical references (p.   ) and index.
    ISBN 0-471-28521-8
    1. Safety education, Industrial. I. Title.
    T55.S13   1994
    658.3'82--dc20   94-6093
                                                CIP

Printed in the United States of America.

10 9 8 7 6 5 4 3 2

The author's experience being that, once all things in life are sorted out and weighed, nothing on this earth matters more than family; he therefore dedicates this book, with love and appreciation, to his wife, Sharon, his mother and father, Joseph and Theresa, and his children, Angela, Sarah, and Meghan.

CONTENTS

FOREWORD

When you invest time in reading a business-related book, you hope for some type of return on your investment. *Developing Safety Training Programs* provides an immediate payback. This may not be obvious in the first chapter, where the author defines the limited yet integral role of safety training within the context of an overall safety program. However, understanding these limitations will focus one's efforts toward the development of *practical and effective* safety training programs.

This book teaches the process of training development. After outlining the process in Chapter 2, subsequent chapters discuss each step in detail. Clear examples illustrate the method necessary to develop a quality training program. The training development process described in this book is very practical. It reflects the experience of someone who has spent many years successfully struggling with safety training development.

Developing Safety Training Programs provides a continual emphasis on safety training as an integral part of an organization. The explanations on how safety training fits into the overall company mission can help the trainer sell the programs to their buyers—the other departments in the company. The final chapter details how to make the sale, explaining how to prepare a cost-benefit analysis for a safety training program. This approach helps training developers to explain their role in supporting the company's mission.

I wish this book had been available many years ago when I started developing safety training programs. It will be required reading for the employees at our consulting firm, which specializes in the development of safety training programs.

Theodore J. Hogan, Ph.D., CIH

Hinsdale, Illinois

P R E F A C E

I once picked up a copy of John Stewart Mill's *On Liberty* at a used-book store. In the first paragraph of the Introduction the editor wrote, "Why reprint [this book] again, . . . At a time when books are so plentiful, and paper so scarce. . . . ?"*

Let's rephrase this question and apply it to *Developing Safety Training Programs*. Is this book worth the paper it is printed on, much less the money spent to purchase it? If the editor of such a noble and notable work as *On Liberty* thought it necessary to begin by justifying the book to the reader, I feel obligated to do the same for *Developing Safety Training Programs*. Why, then, this book? I offer the reader the following rationale.

The Occupational Safety and Health Administration (OSHA) has not been one of the targets of the Clinton Administration's cost-cutting campaign; in fact, the new Administration has increased the agency's budget. This new budget implies a bipartisan commitment to worker safety. The importance of the regulatory mandate for protecting American workers' health steadily increases, no matter what party predominates in Washington. For example, under the previous Republican Administration, OSHA fines were increased sevenfold. New OSHA standards are issued periodically, and when existing standards are revised, they are invariably more rigorous than the ones they replace. Already, over 100 of these standards include provisions for training.

Proposed OSHA reforms will make it easier for the agency to enter into criminal prosecution against management personnel who violate OSHA regulations. Of course OSHA fines, even though they have increased, are an insignificant portion of the total cost of accidents to American industry. These costs have many sources, and are difficult to determine; however, the Rand Institute, a Washington-based think tank, has studied occupational injuries and has estimated these costs at

---

*John Stewart Mill, *On Liberty*. Edited by Alburey Castell. (Northbrook, IL: AHM Publishing Corporation, 1947).

$82 billion per year. Now think what this figure would mean in terms of the U.S. economy: either 2,050,000 Americans could be newly employed, each at $40,000 per year, or the economy could be stimulated by an $82 billion tax cut.

Part of this $82 billion is the cost of worker's compensation, the government mandated insurance program that provides reimbursement to injured workers. Business professionals rank worker's compensation costs as a major motivator for moving their businesses out of the country. Think of the factory closings that might be avoided if worker's compensation costs were a minor expense.

The greatest cost of occupational hazards is the most difficult to measure; the effect of accidents on worker morale, which stands apart from all medical, compensation, and lost-time costs. What is the cost to a company, resulting from a change in attitude, when a worker is injured on the job? How does it affect the morale and attitude of his or her co-workers? Or, to take a more positive tack, what would happen at a typical manufacturing plant if workers were not laboring under the threat of occupational injury? Imagine the immediate beneficial effect on morale, and the resulting long-term effect on productivity.

Finally, consider this ethical perspective. Preventing worker injuries is good—period. It is difficult to imagine a profession that is more personally satisfying than that of developing and implementing successful safety training programs. Safety and health training professionals never wonder, at the end of a hard day, whether their job has any meaning beyond providing income. There is always the satisfaction of considering the accident or illness that did not occur, the pain that was not experienced, the disability that does not exist, the demoralization that never took place, the scar or other disfigurement not present, the cost not incurred, and the anger never elicited by, and manifested against, an employer.

The challenge to American industry has never been greater. There are many areas in which, for generations, the United States was the undisputed leader, where our leadership is now usurped. One of these areas is employee safety. Comparisons between nations are difficult because of differences in injury definitions and reporting strategies, but the results of a recent study, in which the investigators attempted to take such differences into account, appeared to demonstrate that Japanese industry is significantly safer than industry in the United States.

There is no reason for industry in other countries to have this competitive advantage. A safe, healthy working environment *is* achievable—as is currently being proved by many American companies. Safety training, properly developed and focused, can play a significant role in this achievement.

Joseph A. Saccaro

Joliet, Illinois

ACKNOWLEDGMENTS

Tom Lyzenga, Performance Engineer, Ameritech, provided the most thorough critique of the content and structure of the preliminary manuscript. The editorial staff at Van Nostrand Reinhold, in particular Ken McCombs and Alex Padro, initially recommended this project and guided it through completion. The author thanks them all for their encouragement and support.

DEVELOPING
SAFETY
TRAINING
PROGRAMS

THE ROLE OF TRAINING IN THE SAFETY PROGRAM

KEY CONCEPTS OF CHAPTER ONE

*T*he ultimate goal of a safety program is to create an environment in which workers are neither injured nor made ill by the work they perform.

*E*very business needs a safety program, and that program should cover all employees: clerical, administrative, and manufacturing.

*C*ompetent workers (those possessing the knowledge, skills, and motivation to perform their work properly) are likely to be safe workers. Therefore, competency training should be considered a component of a safety program.

A comprehensive safety program affects both the worker (skills, attitudes, and knowledge) and the workplace (administrative controls, engineering controls, workstation design, and protective equipment). Safety training is effective only in addressing skills and knowledge, and may play a small role in attitude. *Many occupational safety hazards are not founded in training-related sources and cannot be alleviated by training.*

■ THE NEED FOR A SAFETY PROGRAM

Every day approximately 80 million Americans go to work. The full-time workers put in, by definition, at least eight hours of work daily; many put in more than that. Part-time workers typically put in at least three hours of work daily. All of these workers are exposed to some risk of injury and illness during the hours that they are on the job. The purpose of occupational safety programs is to eliminate this risk.

This purpose, although noble, is impossible. Risk is inherent to living. It is a reflection of the fact that people are neither omniscient nor infallible. Although safety programs never result in a completely risk-free workplace, a risk-free workplace is the rationale for their existence and the goal toward which they are directed.

Although safety programs cannot eliminate risk, they can go far to reduce it. A safety program is successful to the degree that each worker leaves the job unharmed. Safety professionals find it acceptable for workers to end the working day several hours older. They can be tired and even irritated. They may leave the premises with some new technical or interpersonal skill or with some changed attitudes. This range of attitudes, behaviors, or physical conditions, either positive or negative, is acceptable within the range of a safety program.

The consideration of what is not acceptable may help clarify what is in the acceptable realm. Workers should not be

- *Physically injured.* All their body parts should be attached, undamaged, and in good working order.

- *Emotionally dysfunctional.* They should not be psychologically stressed to the degree that they cannot function normally for the rest of the day, or to a level that their immune system is depressed and they are more susceptible to illness.

- *Predisposed to an injury or illness.* Insulation installers, for example, should not be diagnosed with asbestosis or mesothelioma 20 years after their occupational exposure. Sheet metal workers should not contract severe arthritis because of damage done to their joints during the years that they were employed.

An occupational safety and health program is essential to protecting workers from the injuries listed above, and from innumerable other risks.

Safety does not just happen. The working environment is not inherently safe. Whether manufacturing, consulting, performing clerical tasks, or selling services, the act of working exposes people to certain hazards. Safety training is an important part of the overall safety program. *Important*, in fact, is an understatement. Safety training is *essential*. It is the part of the safety program that is devoted to modifying the behavior of the worker in order to minimize risk. But safety training is *not* the safety program; it is only one part of the program. This is an extremely important point that will be developed and emphasized throughout this book. *Safety training is effective only when all the other elements of an occupational safety training program are in place,* so that all parts can work together to protect the workers from harm. The concept that the overall effect of the interaction of all the parts of a system ("the whole") is greater than the sum of the individual effects of each part is known as *synergism*. Safety program components are highly synergistic.

Because so many factors contribute to worker safety, an accurate safety record is a significant indicator of the overall cultural health of the company. As one safety officer stated, "We know that safety is a clear-cut barometer of organizational excellence. You cannot have an excellent organization that has a lot of accidents. It's an oxymoron."[1]

This book is devoted to providing the reader with the information and techniques needed to develop a quality safety training program—a program that reduces worker risk to levels that the company deems acceptable. But in order to have the perspective necessary to recognize the proper role of training in an occupational safety program, the reader must first have some understanding of all of the components that contribute to occupational safety. To provide that understanding, this first chapter will present a brief overview of all the components of a complete occupational safety program (see Table 1.1). Chapter 2 will summarize every

TABLE 1.1 Components of a Safety Program

▪ Skills	▪ Protective equipment	▪ Workplace written policy
▪ Worker attitudes	▪ Tools	▪ Safety committee
	▪ Training program	

step in the safety training development process. Each remaining chapter will examine and explain each of these steps in detail, with the intent of providing the reader with the knowledge and skills necessary to implement an occupational safety training program.

 ## SAFETY PROGRAM OVERVIEW

Occupational safety programs do work. They can stimulate significant, measurable reductions in a company's accident rate. According to the U.S. Centers for Disease Control, accidents are the number one cause of premature death in the United States;[2] however, the amount that occupational accidents has contributed to this total has been dramatically reduced in recent years. The U.S. Bureau of Labor Statistics records that, over the past 16 years, the number of fatalities per 100,000 full-time workers has decreased by 50 percent, from 9.8 to 4.3.[3] This remarkable statistic is proof that we need not accept occupational injuries as inevitable. Something—regulatory impact, business initiatives, labor initiatives, or a combination thereof—has succeeded in making the American workplace a safer and healthier place.

A healthy workplace is likely to be a *quality* workplace. Quality is one of the most popular buzzwords in today's business world. People often refer to quality or Total Quality Management (TQM) when discussing business trends. One aspect all of these modern quality programs have in common is the concept of *service to the customer*. Customers are defined not only as the end-users of a product, but also as any person(s) whom a worker directly serves. Customers can be internal (for example, members of the company who receive a worker's services) as well as external. The production department is the internal customer of the marketing department, the engineering department is the internal customer of the research department, and so on.

Because every job function contains hazards that can be minimized or eliminated if they are systematically identified and then controlled, all the employees of a company are customers of the safety department. Historically, occupational safety training has focused on industrial workers, but this emphasis is too narrow to ensure a safe workplace, as office workers are also at risk on the job. "According to the U.S. Occupational Safety and Health Administration (OSHA), more than 40,000 disabling injuries and 200 deaths occur in offices each year."[4] The second most costly worker's compensation claim in the United States is for repetitive-motion injury, and many of these claims are made by office, not industrial, personnel who work on office equipment, not heavy machinery.

The key to reducing occupational risk to acceptable levels is to ensure that workers have the skills, attitude, and equipment necessary to do their jobs safely, and that the workplace in which they perform these tasks is designed to minimize worker risk. The worker and the workplace are the two main foci of an industrial safety program. The workplace must be evaluated from the perspective of what hazards it presents to the worker. Hazards must be controllable, and the risk levels must be acceptable to the workers themselves, to regulatory agencies, and to management.

Workers demonstrate certain behaviors that reflect their attitudes about both their jobs and their work-related skills. These skills play as important a role in safety as they do in productivity. According to the *Accident Prevention Manual for Industrial Operations,* "When people are trained to do their job properly, they do it safely."[5] *Competence, safety, and productivity are mutually achievable goals.* One mission of any company's safety personnel is promoting this concept to line management. Often, the time and resources devoted to safety and to the development of competency are viewed as add-on costs of doing business. They should be viewed, and can be portrayed, as highly effective investments. The safety program can be a major contributor to productivity. Healthy workers—on the job and in proper physical and mental condition—are more likely to contribute their best efforts.

Understanding the role that safety training plays in the overall safety program requires that one first understands all the key elements in the safety program, and how each element contributes to protecting workers on the job. When the worker and the workplace are properly matched, workers are unlikely to sustain injury or to develop illnesses. Of course, protecting the safety of the worker often does much to prevent damage to the workplace.

Workers in a properly designed work environment are likely to produce goods and services without damaging the equipment they use, and, because of low anxiety about the risk of injury, are more likely to work effectively. Cost justification will be the theme of Chapter 10, but the cost-effectiveness of a meaningful safety program will be apparent throughout this book. Many safety personnel understand their contribution to their employer's productivity; some, however, feel defensive, as if they are inherently at odds with the people involved with production. There are rare cases when this is true; in these cases, the safety professional is ethically obligated to take a stand that hampers productivity. But those cases are exceptional, and often the problems caused by safe work practices are short-term. Safety professionals, and safety programs, usually make positive contributions to the long-term economic health of the company.

Workers can be affected in many ways by a safety program. The program can directly affect their attitudes, their job skills, and the protective equipment they wear. Other characteristics, such as strength and endurance, can be changed only with great difficulty and only to a limited degree. Other ways that workers cannot be affected—characteristics they possess that are not amenable to change and therefore must be addressed by the work environment—include age, height, and gender.

We will consider each aspect of worker behavior on which an occupational safety program can have an impact.

□ ATTITUDES

Attitude modification constitutes an exciting and challenging part of a safety program. Attitudes can be changed, and, as everyone has observed in himself or herself and others, they do change. But what factors cause them to change, and how these factors may be deliberately manipulated, is far more controversial.

On what safety-related attitudes can safety training have an impact? What can training personnel contribute to inculcating pro-safety attitudes? The answers to these questions are based on many factors, some over which the company has extensive control, some over which it has only limited control, and some over which it has absolutely no influence.

One factor over which individuals have control is their own attitudes. Attitudes are infectious. Safety and training personnel can consciously work at making positive and encouraging statements in an attempt to influence the attitudes of others.

Workers will have an attitude regarding their influence on their workplace. They can view themselves either as being *empowered,* that is, able to make significant changes in their work environment that will reduce the risks associated with the job, or as being *powerless,* that is, unable to change anything important about their work environment. Obviously, workers who perceive themselves as having the ability to control hazards will, out of self-interest, have a better safety record.

Workers may, out of a variety of motives, wish either a positive or negative image for their company. This desire may especially be a factor if the company at-large, or some particular department, is nearing a safety milestone that will result in an award. Group awards are intended to place social pressure on all workers to observe safety rules, but dissatisfied workers may undermine a group's efforts as a way to make a statement about their attitude regarding their company. People enjoy having some control over significant circumstances in their life, and work is certainly one of those circumstances. If workers are not empowered to make positive impacts on the workplace, they may make negative ones. For some individuals, power to undermine or damage something, including a safety record, is preferable to little to no power at all.

Workers may possess attitudes regarding their co-workers that are quite different from those that they possess toward their company as an abstract entity. The *company* may mean management, whereas their co-workers are nonmanagement. Thus, workers who possess bad attitudes about their company may still be motivated to work safely out of a concern for their co-workers. The attitudes conveyed by upper management will have some impact on the workers (though, unfortunately, not always the intended impact); however, the consistent projection of a positive attitude regarding some aspect of work eventually rubs off on others. As one safety officer stated, "We don't pretend to say that we didn't have our skeptics and our cynics in the organization . . . but with the 'total commitment' of top management, quality advocates kept plugging at communication and training."[6]

A company-wide, positive impact on attitude will generally flow from the top down. Occupational safety, industrial hygiene, and occupational health personnel will often find that they have to *sell* the value of their disciplines to decision makers. Often, these personnel cannot assume that the value of their work is self-evident. While this responsibility (selling the value of one's contribution) rests most heavily on supervisory personnel in these departments, nonsupervisory personnel should also see it as a part of their mission.

In terms of occupational safety and health, the most important attitude to promote company-wide is one of personal responsibility for the prevention of accidents and injuries.

☐ SKILLS

Workers may be highly motivated to work safely but still be at risk if they do not have the necessary skills to do the job properly. It is impossible to separate job skills training from safety training, and the wise safety trainers will not so try. Instead, they will accept that job skills and safety are linked, and make sure that skills training incorporates safe practices. Ideally, every skills training program should be submitted to the safety department for review.

In addition to specific job skills, there is one skill that all workers need in order to interact safely with their co-workers—communication skills. Communication skills are rarely addressed at the nonmanagement level, which is a serious mistake based in the failure to recognize the role that poor communication plays in accidents. Major airline accidents, resulting in many deaths and millions of dollars in property losses, have resulted from seemingly slight misunderstandings between air traffic controllers and pilots.

Safe workers are able to effectively communicate information about working conditions to their subordinates, peers, and supervisors, having mastered the techniques for ensuring mutual understanding. Therefore, a successful safety program will contain training in communication skills as well as subject matter expertise.

☐ TOOLS

Safety may begin with the worker, but it extends to every aspect of the job. If workers are to be safe, they must be provided with tools and equipment that allow them to complete the tasks to which they are assigned without causing any acute or chronic bodily or emotional injury.

Tools that do not allow the worker to perform the job are unproductive. Tools that increase the risk of bodily injury are inhumane. For a safety program to be complete, it must include an ergonomic workplace survey, which is a careful and scientific matching of the worker to the tools and job.

Ergonomics is one of the happy areas of industrial safety where the cost-benefit analyses are often easy to perform and the changes easy to justify. This is because the benefits of ergonomically designed workspaces are not limited to reduced accident and illness rates. Comfortable workers, that is, workers who are confident that their jobs are not causing any long-term damage to their bodies, and who are not subject to sprains and strains on the job, are likely to have good morale, be more productive, and produce higher-quality work.

Properly designed tools are a critical component of an ergonomic workspace. In general, they must be designed to minimize the possibility of strain to the workers, electrical shock, and breakage. There are specific rules that apply to various work environments. For example, if tools are to be used in an explosive environment, they must be made of copper, brass, or some other nonsparking alloy.

☐ PROTECTIVE EQUIPMENT

An effective safety program must also ensure that the proper personal protective equipment (PPE) is available. Ideally, PPE should be viewed as a final barrier—a last line of defense between the workers and whatever dangerous substances or energies they deal with. PPE in this situation would be used only as prudent extra protection in the event that other engineering controls fail or good working practices are not followed. Unfortunately, in real-world industrial conditions it is sometimes not technically or financially feasible to eliminate all safety and health hazards, and the PPE is relied on to protect workers from cancer, dermatitis, blindness, burning, and other serious injuries.

Respirators, coveralls, gloves, goggles, hard hats, hearing protection, and other PPE must all be evaluated by their specific effectiveness against the stressors of the work environment in which they will be used, and by the additional stress they generate [which can be significant: for example, protective clothing raises body temperature, especially if the clothing is nonpermeable (as is necessary in many hazardous material responses); respirators make breathing somewhat more laborious; and gloves reduce both tactile sense and dexterity]. The protection offered by this equipment is rather limited. We will look at just two examples of protective equipment: respirators and hearing protection.

Respirators

Aside from air-supplied respirators (which provide the user with an independent source of breathing air), respirators do not compensate for

FIGURE 1.1   Respirators. *(Photo courtesy of 3M Occupational Health and Environmental Safety Division.)*

deficiencies in oxygen. They are designed to protect the user from specific contaminants at relatively low concentrations (see Figure 1.1). If other contaminants are present, or the contaminants for which the respirator was designed are at high concentrations, the respirator's protective capabilities are quickly defeated. Even if a respirator is properly matched to the contaminant and concentration, the seal of a tight-fitting respirator against the face can be easily compromised by a worker's scars, weight changes, and normal aging. Also, both government regulations and common sense mandate that workers be periodically examined to determine whether they are physically capable of wearing a respirator. Even when respirators are properly designed and fitted, workers have to perform with a mask strapped around their face, which is usually uncomfortable and inhibits communication.

Hearing Protection

Hearing protection does not protect against all noise levels at all frequencies. Impact noises, in particular, are not always effectively attenuated by hearing protection. At noise levels about 140 dB, no standard industrial hearing protection provides adequate protection for workers because sound reaches the ear through the body.

Similar limitations exist for other forms of PPE, such as eye and skin protection. Therefore, an effective safety program will include a committee that is continually evaluating hazards to determine if they can be eliminated through changes in equipment or work practices rather than protected against by PPE. When PPE is necessary, the same committee should determine whether it is effective against the hazards for which it was provided, and is accessible to and comfortable for the workers.

☐ SAFETY POLICY

Although at this time there is no legal mandate for a company to have a written safety policy, the Occupational Safety and Health Administration (OSHA) has proposed making a written safety policy mandatory. However, a written policy has many advantages besides anticipating a new law. The safety policy gives the company a consistent structure to follow and provides the company auditors with a tool both for evaluating a department's commitment to safety and for identifying unsafe situations. With a safety policy comes standards (procedures, controls, protective equipment, and the like) that give the safety program substance and meaning (see Table 1.2).

TABLE 1.2   Components of a Safety Policy

■ Audits	■ Accident investigation
■ Controls	■ Hazard reporting and follow-up
■ Protective equipment review	■ Emergency response

The safety policy should also contain clear guidelines on enforcement of safety rules. Like training, enforcement is only one component of a safety program; it is most effective when it works in conjunction with the other elements of the program. Enforcement alone cannot be relied on to motivate employees to comply with safety rules. One reason for this is that it would simply be too expensive. "In an era of leaner organizations and work performed with less supervision, no company can afford to have every employee individually watched by a safety manager."[7]

Another benefit of a written safety policy is that it provides for a formal accident investigation procedure. This ensures that accidents will be systematically investigated; that embarrassing information will not be covered up; and that the "root," or underlying, cause of the accident can be identified. Only when this root cause is identified and remedied can management be confident that the probability of the accident reoccurring has been reduced.

Because no company can be confident that its accident rate will be reduced to zero, a first aid response plan is also an essential part of the overall safety program. This plan should ensure that cardiopulmonary resuscitation (CPR) is available to employees within a few minutes, that minor injuries are properly cared for, and that most major injuries can be stabilized until medical help arrives. Considering the subject-matter expertise involved in developing and teaching a first aid program, and the potential for liability associated with the project, it is advisable to use a nationally recognized program, such as the one offered by the American Red Cross. A company's medical emergency-response program is not limited to training some workers in first aid. There must be provisions for ensuring a reasonable response time from medical professionals. Because of the professional expertise involved in this type of planning, a medical professional should write, or at least review, the emergency response plan.

Summary

Chapter One provides a brief summary of the major elements of an industrial safety program. Safety training plays a limited but extremely important part in making this program successful. The remainder of this book will emphasize analyzing safety hazards to determine whether training can contribute to the remediation of these hazards.

Basically, training can contribute to the resolution of safety problems when, after a careful and systematic analysis of injuries, the researcher determines that the underlying cause of the injuries is a deficiency in skill or knowledge. Training is then an effective means of improving an organization's safety program. Often, however, the identification of skill and knowledge deficiencies as the underlying causes of injuries is incorrect—the result of faulty accident investigation technique.

Training may also assist in correcting safety problems caused by attitude. Most likely, though, attitude problems go deeper into the organizational structure than motivational training can plumb. After the root causes of those attitude problems are corrected, motivational training can be effective in briefly improving attitudes that will then be sustained by organizational policies.

I. Write a list of what you consider acceptable consequences (e.g., employees feel tired) and unacceptable consequences (e.g., employees get injured) of employees putting in a full day's work at your firm.

2. In the last 16 years, the rate of occupational fatalities in the United States has been cut approximately:
   a. 90 percent
   b. by two-thirds
   c. in half
   d. by one-third

3. Write at least five worker characteristics a safety program can change to lower the risk of an injury.

4. Write at least five worker characteristics on which a safety program can have no impact.

5. Write a list of at least five ways a safety program can improve productivity.

6. What are the benefits of having a written safety policy?

7. What are some topics that should be covered in a written emergency response plan?

8. List at least ten variables that should be recorded in an accident documentation program.

9. What are the major components of a corporate safety policy?

10. After identifying a health hazard, what are some of the remedial actions, other than training, that must be addressed?

REFERENCES

1. Stephen Minter, "Creating the Safety Culture," *Occupational Hazards* 53, no. 8 (August 1991):19.

2. "Accidents Top U.S. Premature Deaths," *Safety and Health* (August 1992):58.

3. Douglas E. Robie, letter, *Occupational Hazards* (August 1992):10.

4. Jeanne Stellman and Mary Sue Henifin, *Office Work Can Be Dangerous to Your Health: A Handbook of Office Health and Safety Hazards and What You Can Do About Them* (New York: Pantheon Books, 1983), 1.

5. *Accident Prevention Manual for Industrial Operations,* 7th ed. (Chicago: National Safety Council, 1978), 197.

6. Stephen Minter, "Quality and Safety: Unocal's Winning Combination," *Occupational Hazards* (October 1991):50.

7. "Creating the Safety Culture," *Occupational Hazards,* p. 17.

ELEMENTS OF SAFETY TRAINING DEVELOPMENT

KEY CONCEPTS OF CHAPTER TWO

The training department must have a mission statement derived from the corporate mission statement.

The development of training is a process. Following all the steps in the process ensures a quality product.

◼ OVERVIEW

Chapter 1 presented an overview of an entire industrial safety program. We established that training is an important component of an occupational safety training program, but that its role is limited. As long as safety personnel clearly understand the nature of that role, namely, addressing problems where the primary cause is a deficiency of knowledge or skills, training can be highly effective in reducing the occurrence of occupational illnesses and accidents.

This chapter will provide an overview of the entire process of developing a safety training program. Each succeeding chapter will then take one step in that process and describe it in detail. A reader who carefully completes each chapter, including the application exercises, will possess the necessary skills to develop and implement an occupational safety training program at his or her company.

◼ COMPONENTS OF A SAFETY TRAINING PROGRAM

To ensure focus, the training department, like the safety department, should have a mission statement. The mission statement should provide a guiding concept for members of the training department that makes it clear what their contribution to the corporate mission is. It should also make it clear to members of other departments not only what the role of training is, but also specifically how training contributes to the company's financial health. This is important because training, not being a line function (one that contributes directly to production), is more vulnerable to economic analysis than are those departments directly involved in production.

An essential role of the trainer's job, then, is to defend, both conceptually and financially, the role of the training department to others. The beginning of the conceptual defense is the mission statement.

The following is a sample of a mission statement. If your company has a corporate mission statement, the training department's mission statement should be derived from that.

Establish the Root Causes of Those Hazards

As well as identifying hazards through analyzing tasks, the committee must also establish the "root causes" of those occupational accidents and illnesses. The root cause is the underlying cause—the one that initiated the chain of events that finally resulted in the accident or illness occurring. This is best illustrated by an example, which follows.

> *A box falls on the head of a worker, causing a neck strain. The immediate cause of the injury was the box striking the worker's head. But why did the box fall? It was struck by a forklift. Now we have an underlying cause. Pursuing it further, we determine that the supervisor has frequently ordered the forklift operator to slow down, but there have been no consequences to the driver's ignoring of the orders. Now we have a personnel problem, a lack of enforcement of safety rules—another underlying cause. But before we blame the forklift driver, we need to look at his schedule. Was his work assignment realistic, or did he need to drive as fast as he did in order to complete the work? If so, another underlying cause may have been that he was forced to hurry to meet his supervisor's expectations. Also, why did the bumping of the forklift cause the box to fall? If the boxes were stacked up too high, improper stacking would be another underlying cause.*

In this example, the root causes are the boxes being stacked too high, an unrealistic work schedule for the driver, and a lack of enforcement of company safety policy. The cause was not that the workers involved did not know the policies, so this is not a safety training issue. This is often the case.

There is not necessarily a direct and positive correlation between the knowledge of safety-related rules and safe behaviors. There are many illustrations of this principle in everyday life in the United States. One example is that some sexually transmitted diseases are at near-epidemic levels, although the relationship between sex and disease transmission has been well publicized because of the AIDS crisis. Many private and public agencies promote either abstinence or practices that lower the risk of disease transmission. Most sexually active Americans know of both the risks and the methods for minimizing the risk, yet the majority of sexual exchanges continue to occur with one or both partners unprotected.

The following are other examples that illustrate how knowledge of risks may not lead to safe behaviors:

- Most smokers know they are virtually embracing respiratory disease, yet they continue to smoke.

- People who decline to wear seat belts almost certainly know others who have been needlessly killed, crippled, or disfigured in automobile accidents, yet they do not buckle up.

- Many people who eat a high-cholesterol, high-fat diet are quite knowledgeable about their increased risk of heart disease, yet they do not change their habits.

Changing behaviors can be maddeningly complex. Although training workers about risks may be important, it rarely, in itself, addresses a root cause.

Segregate Those Causes Related to Knowledge or Skills

This book is devoted to safety training. Many of the root causes identified will not be training related. Those that are not training related should be handled appropriately (through engineering controls, administrative controls, or protective equipment). The remaining training-related root causes are the specific performance deficiencies that must be addressed. These must now be stated in a positive fashion, in terms of what knowledge and skills the trainee must possess in order to correct those deficiencies. In other words, safety trainers must define the safe employee as a person with specific skills. Since we want to know whether we are successful in conveying these skills, the skills must be described in measurable terms. Only skills that can be observed can be measured, so those skills must be observable. This step is based on one of the fundamental precepts of safety training: that trainees should not learn safe work practices through trial and error. "Experience is a good teacher, but it gives the examination before the lesson. Exams like these can cause injury, loss of production, increased worker compensation rates, decreased worker morale and decreased profit."[3]

At this point the safety trainer can return to the job hazard analysis, this time reviewing only the sections that have been segregated out in

Job Hazard Analysis

U.S. Department of Labor
Occupational Safety and Health Administration

OSHA 3071
1992 (Revised)

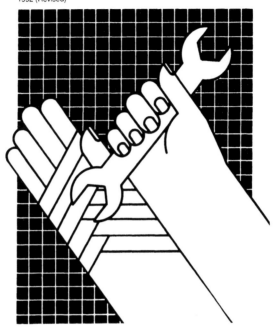

FIGURE 2.1   OSHA offers free literature describing job hazard analysis.

preceding steps. The knowledge needed to perform safely is based on simpler knowledge, or subknowledge. The skills required are likewise based on a series of subskills. Most of these subcomponents will be part of a skill or knowledge hierarchy; that is, the learner needs to know one before he or she goes on to the other. The "tasks"—important components of each job—must be identified, as must the subknowledge and skills from which they are composed. They can be identified through existing job specifications, vendor manuals, and interviews with the employees and their supervisors. Once the tasks and subtasks are identified, the people doing the job should have the opportunity to comment on them. They should be asked to identify any areas that were missed during the development stage, and also to determine which skills can be picked up on the job, which require classroom training, and which require hands-on training. At this point, the workers should also identify the hazards related to each task.

☐ IDENTIFY TRAINING NEEDS

Using the survey of the workers and their supervisors generated by the previous step, select the skills required for training. These would be the skills that, in the opinion of the workers and their supervisors, could not be safely or efficiently picked up on the job. The safety committee should be involved in planning the training at this point. They should review the hazards involved with the tasks and determine which could be eliminated in ways that do not require training (such as engineering or administrative controls). An example of an engineering control would be enclosing a conveyor belt that was transporting some substance that was creating a dust hazard. An example of an administrative control would be reassigning work so that time spent on tasks that could lead to a repetitive-motion injury (like typing) is limited to a specific number of hours per day, with the employee doing other tasks for the remainder of the shift.

☐ IDENTIFY GOALS AND OBJECTIVES

The training developers now know two important things: what skills the workers need to work safely, and which of these skills require training. The next step in the safety program development process is to describe the final product of the training, that is, what the trainee will do on completion of a successful training session. These objectives will describe the action to be performed, the conditions under which the action will take place, and the quality or standard of an acceptable action.

☐ DEVELOP LEARNING ACTIVITIES

Four steps are involved in developing learning activities:

1. Identify the trainees' learning characteristics.

2. Write course evaluation materials.

3. Select or develop instructional materials.

4. Structure the training.

Identify the Trainees' Learning Characteristics

Before we decide what training methods work best, we need to know how the trainees will learn best. The most effective learning methods vary with education, age, attitude, and perception of the work. Let's say that the workers at a particular industry need to set up and use a certain database. Assume that there are two departments that need to be trained. The first (Group 1) is made up of young college graduates whose work requires that they are computer literate. The second (Group 2) consists of older workers who have had only a high school education, and whose job responsibilities have not previously required computer literacy. This situation is common. Many clerical jobs, such as typing and filing, and many industrial jobs, such as machining, now require some knowledge of computer programming.

In this example, the skills the workers need to acquire are the same—setting up and using a database. The training requirements, however, are quite different. Group 1 most likely requires little more than a well-written user's manual. On the other hand, thoughtfully designed, carefully structured training is essential for Group 2. Group 2's training will need to be closely supervised, probably starting with some general familiarization with computer concepts, such as file management and the function of a spread sheet. In this example, the trainees vary drastically in entry skills. They may also vary in need for structure, reading ability, motivation, and so on.

Write Course Evaluation Materials

Once training developers have established goals, objectives, and learning characteristics, they are ready to write the test questions. These should be written from the objectives to ensure that the trainees are evaluated directly on what they need to know for the job, not what the training developers happen to pick up while researching course materials.

Select or Develop Instructional Materials

After identifying the training needs of the work force, writing the objectives, understanding how trainees learn, and writing the test questions, you are ready to select instructional materials. As a safety trainer, you can be confident now that the material you choose will match the training needs of your firm.

Be sure that hands-on skills are matched to hands-on training materials, and that the learning style of your trainees is considered as well as content.

Depending on the available resources, the training developer must choose to either select or develop materials. If no one is able to write a training text, you may need to secure the services of a technical writer. One may be available in another department within the company. If not, it will be necessary to hire an outside professional.

Similar decisions must be made regarding the audiovisuals. Incredible strides have been made in the past years that allow trainers to make beautiful, professional-quality slides, transparencies, and charts without any special skills and at relatively low cost. The same does not hold true for the television medium. Making a training video that is comparable in quality to what people are used to seeing on television requires a substantial investment in specialized tools and equipment. If the quality of the video is not comparable to what people see on television, trainees quickly lose interest.

Structure the Training

Once the training materials are selected or developed, the trainer must decide how to sequence the materials and when to intersperse evaluations and reviews.

The learning style of the trainees is the most critical factor here, although another critical factor is the availability of instructors and resources. This can be a major consideration when you are teaching a hands-on skill for a piece of equipment that is not always available.

There are four approaches to structuring a learning experience:

- Known to unknown

- Simple to complex

- Parts to the whole

- Chronological (same sequence as performed on the job)

We will examine one example of each.

Known to Unknown   Consider the previous example of trainees who previously filed papers by hand and now must do the same work using a computer database. Analogies can be drawn from their previous job that will help them comprehend their new one. For example, the hard drive is the file drawer, the data are the files, the database program is the filing procedure, and the volume of the data (files) determines how many will fit on the hard drive (file drawer).

Simple to Complex   American Red Cross adult cardiopulmonary resuscitation (CPR) is an excellent example of a training program that incorporates multiple structuring techniques. One technique used is ensuring that trainees master simpler, easier-to-learn skills first, then move on to more complex skills. Trainees first learn how to identify breathing emergencies, then cardiac emergencies. They learn rescue breathing and airway-clearing techniques for adults in normal situations, then move on to special situations such as obesity and pregnancy. Finally they learn CPR, the most complex of the skills included in the course. The progression from simple to complex skills is gradual and carefully structured. Competency must be demonstrated at each level before trainees move on to the next.

Parts to the Whole   Hazardous material spill response requires a number of physical skills, such as using a self-contained breathing apparatus and donning and doffing protective equipment. It also requires cognitive skills such as interpreting analytical instruments and hazard communication resources. These are typically taught separately, in the appropriate learning environment. Then the parts are combined in a simulated hazardous material spill response drill.

Chronological   For some jobs, the sequence of the tasks to be performed is one of the most difficult aspects of the job to master. This is often the case in highly procedural work (for example, a bank teller). A chronological training structure is effective for this type of work because

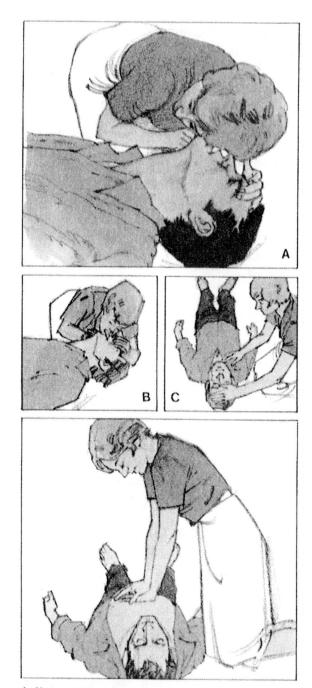

A. Airway open
B. Breathing restored
C. Circulation checked

FIGURE 2.2   American Red Cross CPR training incorporates multiple
learning techniques, including moving from simple
to complex skills.

it affords a trainee the opportunity to practice the proper sequence of tasks.

☐ CONDUCT THE TRAINING

At last! The program is finally presented to the trainees. The instructor should have the presentation skills necessary for the course, such as the ability to operate the audiovisual equipment, tools, machinery, or other equipment used during the hands-on portion. If the course includes a lecture, the instructor must have the ability to speak clearly and articulately in front of a group, to ask open-ended questions, and to guide learning.

As a general rule, all training should begin with a review of the program's learning objectives, so that the trainees know what is expected of them. Those objectives should be related to the values of the trainees, so that the trainees know what the instructor's expectations are and are motivated to learn.

All training presentations should be interactive. The trainees should have the opportunity to be exposed to information and then to demonstrate whether they understand the information. This sequence of taking in, then demonstrating understanding of, information is essential to the learning process. The interactive environment necessary for this to take place is also required by OSHA's definition of training:

> *The planned and organized activity of a consultant to impart skills, techniques and methodologies to employers and their employees to assist them in establishing and maintaining employment and place of employment which is safe and healthful.*[4]

Training should take place prior to the final examination for the class; it should be part of the learning process.

☐ EVALUATE PROGRAM EFFECTIVENESS

The effectiveness of any training program is determined by the performance of the trainees. Plan to systematically and thoroughly evaluate the pilot program. Solicit evaluations from the trainees, from the instructors, and from the trainees' supervisors. Determine if the training is making a meaningful change to the trainees' performance on the job.

If the trainees are to be evaluated during the pilot program, it is a good idea to inform them that the results of the evaluation will not be part of any permanent record and will not be used as criteria for any decisions regarding their career. The first program will not run as smoothly as the subsequent programs, and it is not fair to penalize trainees for your problems with the presentation.

Ideas for improving the program should be solicited from any people who have the experience to offer constructive criticism. This will include, at a minimum, the instructors, the trainees, and the trainees' supervisors who are in a position to observe on-the-job behavior changes. Every phase of the training program must be held up to evaluation, not just the behavior of the trainees. The course objectives should be periodically evaluated to ensure that they still address the current safety issues in the company.

The personnel who make the recommendations may or may not be in a position to evaluate and implement the changes.

☐ IMPROVE THE PROGRAM

As much as possible, within the constraints of the course objectives, incorporate the suggestions of the instructors, trainees, and supervisors. Compare the students' performance to the desired performance, and change content, learning aids, and structure as needed.

The personnel are valuable sources of ideas for improving the quality of the program. A system must be in place for soliciting their recommendations, for evaluating the recommendations with the intent of selecting, and for implementing the best recommendations. Part of this system should be a tracking procedure that ensures that once a recommendation is made, it is evaluated by the proper people. Quite possibly, depending on the size of the organization, the people doing the evaluating and the people doing the tracking will not be the same.

The initiators of new ideas must be informed of the progress that has been made. If their idea is rejected, they should be given an explanation as to why. If it is accepted, they should be congratulated.

Summary

Congratulations! You have now created an interesting, cost-efficient course that meets a clearly determined corporate need and is tailored to the learning style of your trainees. You are keeping your co-workers healthy, saving the company money, and (it is hoped) having fun.

The remaining chapters will clarify and expand on each component of the safety program development process so that the reader will be able to develop his or her own safety training program.

1. List the key components in the training development process, and give a one-sentence definition of each.

2. What are the purposes of a mission statement?

3. Write a mission statement for your training organization.

4. What are the three steps involved in determining if training is needed?

5. Circle the components that belong in your company's mission statement
   a. How the training department ties in to the company mission statement
   b. A detailed program for accomplishing the training department's mission
   c. Previous successes of the training department
   d. The purpose of the training department
   e. Short- and long-term training department goals
   f. A brief general statement of how the training department's mission is accomplished

6. What is the first step in the training development process?
   a. Selecting a training program
   b. Presenting the case for training to upper management
   c. Performing a cost-benefit analysis of training
   d. Determining if training is needed

7. Job hazard analysis includes a review of (circle two):
   a. Historical data on accidents
   b. Employee attitudes regarding safety
   c. The safety programs of other companies
   d. The tasks that make up employee job responsibilities

8. What might be the "root cause" of an employee dislocating his shoulder after slipping on a wet floor?
   a. There was no barrier tape around the puddle.
   b. The employee was never trained in hazard awareness.
   c. The floor was wet.
   d. The ceiling leaked during a rainstorm.

9. Write a definition of *root cause*.

10. Training goals should describe _____ and _____ behaviors.
   a. Focused, easy to learn
   b. Training-related, safe
   c. Reasonable, safety-oriented
   d. Measurable, objective

11. Give at least five resources that can be consulted when identifying training tasks.

12. Trainee test questions should be developed from:
    a. Equipment manuals
    b. Learning objectives
    c. The job hazard analysis
    d. Training materials

13. What are the three components of an objective?

 # REFERENCES

1. Stephen Minter, "Quality and Safety: Unocal's Winning Combination," *Occupational Hazards* (October 1991):47.

2. "Training Requirements in OSHA Standards and Training Guidelines," in *Occupational Hazards* (OSHA Publication 2254, August 1991).

3. Bruce E. Everett, "Training Techniques That Work Within an Integrated Safety Program, *Professional Safety* (May 1989): 34.

4. OSHA 29 CFR 1908.2 (Definitions).

DETERMINING IF TRAINING IS NEEDED

KEY CONCEPTS OF CHAPTER THREE

*J*ob hazard analysis, the process of (1) breaking all jobs down to their component tasks, (2) identifying the hazards associated with those tasks, and (3) determining the best way to mitigate those hazards, is the heart of an industrial safety program.

*E*ffective job hazard analysis requires the support and cooperation of both supervisors and the people who perform the tasks. Their experience is required for both identifying and mitigating hazards.

*S*afety training personnel must listen carefully to "problem workers," those with a perceived attitude problem. The true problem may be with the safety program.

When discussing a process that consists of a series of interdependent steps, such as the process of developing a safety training program, making a case that one part is more important than another is about as meaningful as a "Which came first, the chicken or the egg?" argument. Every step in the safety training development process is critical to the quality of the final product, that is, the behaviors that the trainee demonstrates on the job.

The process of determining if training is needed consists of:

- Identifying safety and health hazards

- Establishing the root causes of those hazards

- Segregating those causes related to knowledge and skills

 ## FUNDAMENTALS OF JOB HAZARD ANALYSIS

Identifying safety and health hazards is the first step in the safety training development process. It affects far more than safety training; it is crucial to every component in the safety program—engineering controls and administrative policies as well as safety training.

The key to identifying safety and health hazards and establishing their root causes is called *job hazard analysis*. Job hazard analysis is the product of the best minds in the field of safety and health. It is an element in every nationally recognized safety program, and it has a stunning record of success.

Job hazard analysis presents a practical method for identifying occupational hazards, and it is the foundation for determining the best course for correcting those hazards. It provides the documentation trainers need to convince upper management that they have selected the proper course of action. Should a company's safety program be audited by OSHA, the job hazard analysis would provide valuable documentation that the safety program matches the needs of the workers.

The steps of job hazard analysis are as follows:

1. Determine the steps involved in each job.

2. Identify safety hazards related to each task.

3. Determine the best way to remediate those hazards.

We will define a job as a group of related responsibilities assigned to one worker. Each of those responsibilities is broken into tasks. A task is defined as a behavior, initiated by a cue (something that elicits the task) that has a discrete beginning and an end and that results in a meaningful product or service. The cue could be the previous step in the process or some action that signaled that the process should begin. If a behavior does not result in a meaningful product or service, it is not a task. Tying your shoes is a task; making the loops is not. Making the loops is a task component that contributes to completion of the task.

There are a number of sources for determining the steps involved in a job: the people doing the job, operation manuals, repair manuals, company policy documents, and written procedures. Every source has its own benefits and liabilities. If the safety training is to be comprehensive, it is necessary to use all of the sources.

The people doing the job, and their supervisors, are the best sources of information about the steps involved in doing the job, but these sources probably are not the first ones to check. They generally will need an outline of the job to jog their memory.

The best place to start might be a written description of the work, such as a company procedure manual. This can be supplemented where necessary by vendor manuals that describe the maintenance and operation of machinery used in the job. These written sources may give a fairly accurate description of the work, but for the following reasons they will never be perfectly accurate:

Workers will have improvised methods to make the job easier, or to improve speed or production.

Machinery and software may have been modified or upgraded since they were installed. Current procedures may not reflect these upgrades.

No job is completely described on paper. There will be many legitimate, job-related activities that workers engage in that are not described anywhere. Some of these activities will involve risks that will not be identified unless workers are interviewed.

Once a job description has been roughed out using the above references, the training developer should spend several days, or as much time as feasible, walking around with the workers, taking notes on what they do, and asking them about the procedures they perform, the processes they follow, and the equipment they operate and repair. Of course, many people would not be immediately open to having someone follow them around, taking notes on what they do. Success in this venture requires that the training developer cultivate a rapport with the employees who are being observed. Three "ground rules" will help the trainer establish that rapport:

1. It must be clear to the workers being observed that the safety trainer is not there for evaluation of workers' efficiency. Observation for the purpose of learning and observation for the purpose of evaluation do not mix. Even one violation of this rule is enough to seriously and permanently damage the credibility of the safety trainer and, by implication, a firm's safety program.

2. The workers should be trained in the fundamentals of job hazard analysis. They will be far more cooperative if they understand the crucial role they play in improving worker safety.

3. Very likely, information will come out about safety hazards during the observation part of the program. Have a procedure in place for processing this information into the system for correcting safety hazards. Make sure any recommendations are tracked and that the person making the recommendations is notified of the outcome. Ensure that the people with the expertise to correct problems are aware that the problems exist. Often they may offer a solution not related to training. For example, in identifying hazardous chemicals, "approximately 30% of employers would have replaced a hazardous chemical with a less hazardous one because of information provided to them under the [Hazardous Communications] regulation."[1]

After a draft of the job description has been formulated, it should be reviewed by the people who know the job best—the supervisors and the workers. That group should review the draft and recommend where tasks should be condensed or broken into more steps. They should also

TABLE 3.1   Safety Training Survey

Task	Formal Training?	Type of Training	Risk Involved
	Y N	Classroom Hands-on On the job	H M L

recommend additional tasks if they know of any that are not included in the original job description. Prior to analyzing the job description in this fashion, the group must be trained in the fundamentals of job hazard analysis and in the concepts of "job," "task," and "task analysis," so that they understand the process of identifying job responsibilities and breaking those responsibilities into tasks.

The next draft should be a concise and quite thorough description of the job to be analyzed for safety and health hazards. Once again, the workers doing the job, and their supervisors, are best qualified to do this. They should rate each task as to whether it can be learned on the job or whether it requires formal training. The amount of risk involved with the task should also be rated. Table 3.1 shows an example of a safety training survey.

Have as many workers as feasible fill out this survey. Do not assemble the best workers for this; it is necessary to get a cross section that represents the actual worker population with regard to competency and range of skills. In fact, the "problem workers" have a special role in this type of survey. Let's consider two distinct groups of "problem" (higher than average incidence of accidents) workers: those with poor health and those with a poor attitude.

Before the advent of sophisticated electronic monitors, miners used to take parakeets down into the mines with them. Because the birds are much more sensitive than are humans to toxic gases, the birds would collapse when the level of those gases began to rise, providing an early warning system for the miners.

A safety expert has pointed out that the physically weak employee acts, in a sense, like that little parakeet. If there is some stressor in the workplace, the employees who have the least resistance to injury and disease are likely to be the first ones to show evidence of that stressor. If the workers who are overweight and out of shape are suffering back injuries, the smart supervisor will try to eliminate the root cause of that injury. This is one of those happy situations where the humane action and the most productive action are coincidental. Designing the job so that the marginal health worker stays healthy will ensure that the stronger workers also stay healthy. Weak supervisors will complain that they are forced to pay for the consequences of the accident victim's poor physical condition. This is, to a partial extent, true. In some cases companies do bear the burden of health problems that are not occupationally related. But whereas the weak supervisor will complain about this situation, the smart supervisor will address the problem by promoting health awareness in the workplace.

The workers with a bad attitude can be viewed in the same light. They are the ones who are most sensitive to emotional stressors in the workplace, just as physically weak workers are the ones most sensitive to physical stressors. Complaining about workers with a bad attitude only damages morale. If the company has a fair, objective evaluation system, then there should be some way of measuring attitude problems and eventually justifying the termination of that individual. But a smart supervisor can take a positive approach and try to identify the occupational stressors that contribute to the bad attitude (even though acknowledging that many of the causes of the attitude may not be occupational) and eliminate those stressors wherever possible.

In summary, safety trainers should assertively correct the problems they have the authority or resources to correct. Sometimes that will mean partial solutions to training and performance problems. The world is a highly imperfect place and will remain so in spite of everyone's best efforts.

Once the job description has been written and revised by people intimately familiar with the actual work, it still needs to be further revised based on a review of additional databases related to worker safety and health. The historical accident record is the most important of these. Individual accidents should be analyzed to determine the contributing factors, with particular attention paid to how those factors are related to the job description. Accident trends must also be analyzed because these are the best indicators that some remedial action is required in the workplace. Finally, the victims of accidents should be interviewed for their views on the causes of accidents and for their suggestions on remedial actions that will minimize the possibility of reoccurrence.

Job competency has a major role in safety. A technically competent worker will probably have an excellent safety record. A safety officer states, "We all know that you can have the best plant in the world, but if you don't have the people properly trained to operate it, you can get into trouble. [If the company] took the approach in teaching its new employees how to perform their jobs correctly, it would be teaching them how to work safely."[2]

RED FLAGS FOR SAFETY TRAINING

In addition to the type of surveying described above, there are a number of other "red flags" for safety training that do not necessarily mean that training should be performed, but that it should be considered.[3] Table 3.2 and the following sections in this chapter present the various red flags for safety training.

NEW EMPLOYEES

A safe assumption is that new employees do not start the job with the proper attitudes and knowledge regarding safety on the job. Instruct them while they are still fresh and open to learning. Do not allow them to do any work for which they are not trained. Employees will begin acquiring attitudes from their co-workers from the first day. Turn that phenomenon into a benefit by ensuring they pick up the correct attitudes.

NEW EQUIPMENT

Any new equipment should be carefully scrutinized for safety hazards, preferably before it is purchased. Even office equipment can be dan-

TABLE 3.2 Red Flags for Safety Training

New employees	New equipment
New processes	Rising accident rates
Rising insurance rates	Errors in operating or manufacturing
Expansion or contraction of the company	

gerous. (In 1991, 200 office workers died from occupational injuries!) Of course, much industrial equipment is more hazardous than office equipment.

☐ NEW PROCESSES

Even if workers are using the same equipment as they have in the past, processes for using this equipment may change. With new processes, as with anything unfamiliar, come new hazards.

☐ RISING ACCIDENT RATES

This is an obvious indicator of the need for job hazard analysis. If accidents are on the rise, causes must be identified and analyzed. Accident rates will not be noticed unless accident statistics are carefully and accurately maintained. Documentation of accidents is required by OSHA; employers must maintain an "OSHA 200" log that records basic information regarding accidents. The minimum data needed to satisfy OSHA requirements is probably not adequate for any but the smallest businesses that wish to monitor accident trends. The following is information that would be helpful to the safety trainer looking for possible training needs:

- Location of accident

- Job title

- Possible causes

- Remedial actions

- A brief description of the accident by the victim

- Gender

- Protective equipment

This sort of record keeping requires a database so that safety trainers and other interested personnel can sort information by the variables in which they are interested.

For example, let's say that an instructor wished to determine whether accident rates were rising among male maintenance workers on the afternoon shift at a company's midwestern manufacturing plants. If an accident database is set up with separate "fields" (areas for storing information) for gender, job title, shift, and location, it would be a simple task, probably requiring only a few minutes, to generate a report tracking that particular group's accident record over time. Without a database that same report might take hours or days. The safety trainer will be much more likely to identify accident trends if a database is available.

☐ RISING INSURANCE RATES

Most insurance firms will send loss-control specialists out to determine if a site is insurable. These people are a valuable resource to safety trainers. While loss-control specialists are trained to determine if engineering controls (not safety training programs) meet established standards, they are generally very knowledgeable regarding both safety regulations and the recommendations of expert groups such as the American Society of Safety Engineers, the National Institute of Occupational Health and Safety, and the American Fire Protection Institute.

☐ ERRORS IN OPERATING OR MANUFACTURING

This includes all errors, even if they are not safety related. The purpose of a company is to produce a quality product or service. That requires a quality working environment, and the safety staff is more important to a quality working environment than any other group. Defective parts are an indication that there is a breakdown of process somewhere along the manufacturing or service delivery line. This is enough evidence to make the safety trainer at least suspect that safety-related processes may also be breaking down.

☐ EXPANSION OR CONTRACTION OF THE COMPANY

Probably no economic activity is as gut-wrenchingly stressful as "downsizing," reducing the work force through forced retirement, firing, layoffs, and attrition. This type of stress is often an indicator of safety problems to come. On or off the job, overstressed people are accident prone. An expansion of the work force also generates stress and possibly some confusion. New people will be brought in, and probably new responsibilities will be created. In both cases, the work force will be exposed to new hazards, some of which may be alleviated by safety training.

☐ JOB HAZARD ANALYSIS IN RESPONSE TO "RED FLAGS"

Sometimes multiple red flags can pop up, indicating the need for a job hazard analysis. At one company, one piece of equipment was undergoing a higher-than-normal rate of failure (one red flag), apparently due to operator error, and there had been a near-accident—an employee narrowly avoided a chemical burn (a second red flag). The company's training department did not immediately institute refresher training on the safe and proper operation of the equipment. Instead, training department and operating personal analyzed the circumstances leading to the equipment malfunctions and the near-accident. They concluded that some of the instrumentation that indicated the operating status of the equipment was out of service, and some was not working accurately. Operators used this instrumentation when making decisions about the equipment's operation, and they were making those decisions based on incorrect or missing information.

The resultant problems were a classic case of "GIGO" (garbage in–garbage out). The faulty information resulted in incorrect operation. The personnel who analyzed the problem submitted requests for the instrumentation to be repaired. After the repairs were completed, the reliability of the equipment was restored, and no more accidents, or "close calls," occurred.

Performing a job hazard analysis, instead of doing "knee-jerk" training, restored both equipment reliability and safety. Once the hazards have been identified, the root, or underlying, causes of those hazards must be ferreted out. A list should be made of all the possible causes of each hazard, and then a committee of experienced employees, including representatives from both labor and management, should select those causes that can be directly related to the hazard, and define them precisely. Safety training developers who determine the need for training by conducting a systematic job hazard analysis can be confident as they continue in the training development process. They have a rationale for the development of those programs that is both ethical and economically sound.

1. What are the three components of determining if training is needed?

2. Write a definition of job hazard analysis that includes its three major components.

3. What are the groups that would have valuable suggestions in determining the tasks involved in a job?

4. What are the written sources that would include the tasks involved in a job?

5. Why are written sources alone not adequate?

6. What are the sources that can be checked to identify the hazards related to a specific job?

7. What are some "red flags" that should indicate that safety training is needed?

8. How can "problem workers" be used to identify safety hazards?

9. Give an example where safety training would play a major role in mitigating a safety hazard.

10. Give an example where an engineering control would play a major role in mitigating a safety hazard.

 # REFERENCES

1. "News," *Occupational Health and Safety* (July 1992):11.

2. Stephen Minter, "Quality and Safety: Unocal's Winning Combination," *Occupational Hazards* (October 1991): 47.

3. "Safety Training," Chapter 9, in *Accident Prevention Manual for Industrial Operations,* 7th ed. (Chicago: National Safety Council, 1978), 197.

IDENTIFYING TRAINING NEEDS

KEY CONCEPTS OF CHAPTER FOUR

*S*afety and health hazards, once identified, must be eliminated or mitigated. This may be accomplished by engineering controls (changing equipment), administrative controls (changing policy or procedures), or protective equipment. Any of these three components may require training.

*M*any safety hazards and performance problems are not directly related to lack of skills or knowledge.

*E*ffective training must address the cognitive (mental), psychomotor (hands-on), and affective (attitudinal) domains of learning.

OVERVIEW

There is a popular saying that identifying a problem is half the work of creating a solution. If that were true, the safety training developers would be 50 percent finished with the development process, because in completing the job hazard analysis, they have successfully identified the problem activities at the work site. Unfortunately, the saying does not hold true for developing safety training programs: the training program is far from 50 percent complete. In fact, development activities have not even begun; only predevelopment research has been done.

On a positive note, the completed job hazard analysis is a solid foundation for the training development activities to come. It is also the foundation for many other aspects of the safety program, including the selection of engineering and administrative controls. Using the job hazard analysis as a guide, the developer can now select the most cost-effective solution to a given safety problem. The developer is also way ahead of any company that tries to improve its safety program without first performing a job hazard analysis, because the analysis indicates exactly where money, time, and resources need to be concentrated.

However, the developer does not yet know what specific type of resources are needed to correct the identified problems. The best method for determining this is to review the recommendations of the personnel who completed surveys as part of the job hazard analysis. There are also other approaches that will help determine the best approach to a given problem. According to one consultant, "Sixty to 80 percent of the problems people ask me to solve don't turn out to be related to lack of skills or knowledge. Instead, they involve [other] performance barriers." Consequently, it is important not to assume that a training solution exists.[1] She further states, "[S]tart with the worst-possible-case assumption—that classroom training is not worth its cost—and then [try] to find ways to avoid it and still get the desired results."[1]

While this book emphasizes the role of safety training in improving an organization's safety record, it is written from the perspective that there are often other, better solutions to safety problems, such as engineering or administrative controls. Those options will be examined in this chapter, but first, the process of establishing training content and the limitations of that training will be discussed.

CONTENT OF TRAINING PROGRAMS

American workers are protected on the job by OSHA, which stands for both a body of law (the Occupational Safety and Health Act) and a federal agency (the Occupational Safety and Health Administration). Many of the standards within the OSH Act require that employees be trained prior to initiating certain types of work, and that they be periodically retrained. Sometimes the frequency of this retraining is not specified, but most often annual retraining is recommended. Occasionally, more frequent training is required. Fire brigades, for example, must be trained quarterly. The OSH Act is a federal law, not merely a set of recommendations. A company is liable for hefty fines for not complying with its mandates. In fact, company personnel are even liable for criminal prosecution for disregarding OSHA statutes. This is not merely an academic issue. OSHA has successfully pursued criminal prosecution of executives at companies where serious health and safety violations have occurred. Lower-level management personnel have also been prosecuted under OSHA, although this is less common. (Still, even if safety and training personnel are not at much personal risk for going to jail, who wants to have to visit their boss at the "big house" for a performance evaluation?) OSHA reform legislation would make criminal prosecution much more common. Although this reform legislation did not pass during the previous Republican Administration, it will certainly be reconsidered, and probably supported, by the Clinton Administration.

Some states have state-level OSHA agencies with provisions that go well beyond the federal ones. State OSHA rules are just as much law as federal ones, with the same consequences for violations.

OSHA publishes a booklet, *OSHA Requirements in OSHA Standards and Training Guides,* which summarizes all the training provisions in OSHA law. It can be obtained from the U.S. Department of Labor and is updated annually. Table 4.1 lists the ten most common OSHA citations from the general industry standard.

Apart from the financial and legal repercussions of noncompliance with OSHA regulations, there are other good reasons to include these regulations in a company's training program. These laws were written in response to instances of American workers being injured and killed on the job. While businesses sometimes object to the specific wording of an OSHA standard, there is little written in occupational safety and health

TABLE 4.1   Ten Most Common OSHA Citations from the General Industry Standard

Standard	Description
1200 (h)	Hazard communication employee information and training
1200 (e) (1)	Providing a written hazard communication program
5 (a) (1)	General—not providing a safe workplace
212 (a) (1)	Providing guards for moving machinery
1200 (g) (1)	Providing Material Safety Data Sheets
215 (b) (9)	Proper adjustment of abrasive wheel guards
219 (d) (1)	Providing guards for pulleys
151 (c)	Providing eyewash stations
212 (a) (3) (ii)	Providing guards for moving machinery at the point of operation
147 (c) (1)	Written energy control program

literature stating that OSHA-mandated training requirements are unnecessary or generally unreasonable.

The goal of a safety trainer is maintaining the health and safety of workers on the job, not avoiding citations. Training merely to avoid citations will not decrease the rate and severity of injuries, nor does it satisfy the spirit of the law. While an effective, properly designed safety training program will keep a company in compliance with the law, the inverse is not necessarily true; a training program that ensures compliance is not necessarily properly designed and effective. Over 100 current OSHA standards contain some requirement for training. Companies can buy training programs that cover all, or nearly all, of those requirements. The programs are carefully designed to include all the information OSHA requires them to include, but they do not protect workers. Only systematically identifying and addressing safety hazards can do that.

If, on comparing OSHA training requirements to their company's job hazard analysis, safety trainers conclude that some requirement is particularly inappropriate to their company, the safety trainers should request an interpretation from an attorney well versed in occupational law. It is possible that the regulations do not apply to the company. The OSHA standard is far from user friendly and can be easily misinterpreted. If the attorney confirms that the regulations apply, there is another option available if an OSHA training requirement does not seem reasonable. OSHA will sometimes issue a "variance"—permission to disregard a portion of the standard. Obtaining a variance is time consuming, and the company must make a persuasive case. Once it is clear that an

OSHA, Environmental Protection Agency (EPA), or other legal requirement applies to a company, it may be best to consider it as nonnegotiable and devote one's time and energy to compliance.

While legally mandated training is an important component in a company's safety training program, it is not the foundation of the program. The authors of the various labor and environmental laws do not know your employees, your procedures, your manufacturing processes, or your product. There are sure to be major gaps in your safety training program if the training department's goal is merely to protect the company from citations for noncompliance with government safety regulations. On the other hand, there is every reason to expect a dramatic improvement in safety if the department's goal is to address all the hazards identified in the job hazard analysis. The job hazard analysis that was described in Chapter 2, not OSHA regulations, is the foundation of successful safety training. The training must include, but should not be limited by, all relevant OSHA requirements.

If a company's worker's are to remain safe and healthy, the hazards identified in the job hazard analysis must be addressed. Here is where safety training may play an important role. But before planning training, first consider the efficacy of safety training as opposed to other solutions to occupational hazards. *Safety training is often an ineffective method of addressing safety and health hazards.*

Training, if used appropriately, can also be a marvelous method of problem solving. Training personnel are motivated to remain in the training function when they observe the alleviation of organizational problems through changes in human behavior that result from a training program. The look of self-assurance on the face of an employee who has just mastered a new skill, be it CPR or interpersonal communication, provides most training personnel with a nonmeasurable, but nevertheless highly gratifying, job benefit. That being the case, why are trainers advised to find other solutions to safety problems? There are several excellent reasons.

- *Training is expensive.* The cost of training may be easier to hide than the cost of new equipment or facilities because the people are already there. It is easier to hide worker hours than machines in a budget. But the expense, even if elusive, is nonetheless real. Training is time taken away from production; training facilities must be clean and attractive (that is, cost a lot) for training to work; and training requires a substantial investment in audiovisual supplies. What's more, training must be reinforced, which means it must be periodically repeated. If the exact same program is repeated time after time, trainees quickly get bored, and bored trainees are not in a learning mode. Avoiding this problem requires continual development of the training program to convey the necessary knowledge and skills in a variety of ways. This continual training program development requires the time and energy of bright, knowledgeable, enthusiastic employees whose energies are then diverted from production.

- *Training may be ineffective.* Training can be effective when the trainees are properly motivated and when the training has been well designed to focus on the needed behaviors. But that situation is rarely the case in safety training. Most of the time, not everyone is sold on safety training. Managers have been selected and then promoted for their ability to maintain production in spite of the plethora of nonproduction-related responsibilities with which they must deal. Although they *should* view safety as an ethical mandate, they don't always. Nonmanagement employees may view safety rules as one more factor that decreases their comfort level and increases their frustration level on the job.

- *Training can undermine morale.* Effective training, successfully completed, is a great morale builder. Unfortunately, the inverse is also true; poorly planned or executed training programs often devastate employee morale. If employees report safety hazards and those hazards are not addressed by a safety committee or some other group within the company, or if workers observe co-workers being repeatedly injured by uncorrected hazards, safety training alone will increase, not decrease, the overall level of employee cynicism. Safety meetings and safety training will be quite hard on the personnel attempting to run them.

Training has a critical role in an occupational safety program. This book is dedicated to ensuring that safety training is effective. It is important, though, for safety personnel to remember that when safety training is moved out of that limited arena where it works properly, it becomes expensive and ineffective and is a detriment to safety on the job.

TABLE 4.2 Nontraining Options for Minimizing Occupational Hazards

Engineering controls
Specialization
Administrative controls
Protective equipment

Following are four nontraining approaches to correcting the safety hazards identified in the job hazard analysis. They are presented in order of their effectiveness (see Table 4.2). Remember that "effective" does not mean "feasible" or "affordable"; that is why the first, and most effective, technique is not always used.

NONTRAINING APPROACHES TO CORRECTION OF SAFETY HAZARDS

ENGINEERING CONTROLS

An engineering control, a physical change to the workplace, is the first and best way to mitigate a safety hazard. For example, if a worker is exposed to excessive dust during a cleaning job, the installation of a local ventilation system that directs the dust away from the worker's breathing zone would be an engineering control. Changing the cleaning process so that the product was cleaned in a wet state, eliminating dust emissions, would also be an engineering control.

If workers are suffering from back strain during the moving of stock, and the job is redesigned so that mechanical assistance is available, perhaps in the form of a power forklift that lifts the boxes or a rolling conveyor that pushes them, the forklift or conveyor would be considered an engineering control.

Engineering controls are the ideal solution to safety hazards. In some cases, like the ventilation system, they require no attitudinal or behavior changes on the part of the worker who benefits from them. In other cases, such as providing the forklift, some new worker skills are necessary, but workers are strongly motivated by their increase in personal comfort to learn the new behaviors.

Often, engineering controls are morale builders. When workers see new equipment installed that will improve their chances of leaving the workplace uninjured, they are more likely to be relaxed and able to concentrate on the job. Also, they see management taking responsibility for safety. On the other hand, when workers are training to avoid a hazard, they may think that management is telling them that they are responsible for injuries related to that hazard. They may not believe that is reasonable or fair.

Also, engineering controls may improve productivity. The same hazard that was causing injuries may have been hampering production and was almost certainly raising the stress level of the workers.

Another benefit of engineering controls is that they are often one-time investments, unlike training, which has to be periodically repeated.

As with any new equipment, installation of a new engineering control may make some additional training necessary, but this will likely be training to impart technical proficiency. Technical training is generally easier to implement and evaluate than is safety training.

Some OSHA regulations require that engineering controls be considered first when addressing safety hazards. Regulation 29 CFR 1910.134 (Respiratory Protection), for example, states that "[i]n the control of those occupational diseases caused by breathing air . . . the primary objective shall be to prevent atmospheric contamination. This shall be accomplished as far as feasible by accepted engineering control measures."[2]

Unfortunately, engineering controls are not always feasible. Where and when they are not, the second-best alternative for addressing safety hazards is specialization.

☐ SPECIALIZATION

The second approach to be considered when minimizing job hazards is the use of specialists, either internal or external. Asbestos abatement work is a good example of work where specialized workers help minimize the risk. Asbestos abatement requires a great deal of training, record keeping, and medical monitoring. If this work is identified on the job hazard analysis, management may choose to hire a firm that specializes in this type of work, or they may choose to select a small group of employees and assign this group to all asbestos abatement jobs.

☐ ADMINISTRATIVE CONTROLS

Administrative controls, the third approach, reduces or eliminates a hazard by changing a procedure. Consider the two examples given previously: a worker exposed to unhealthy levels of dust, and workers suffering from back strains and sprains from moving heavy equipment.

For the first example, assume that, because of the nature of the product, cleaning it in a wet state is not feasible. And because of the setup in the facility, local exhaust ventilation would be impossible to install. Two administrative controls might be used to protect workers from high levels of dust:

1. *Job rotation:* Workers' time on the job could be limited so that no single worker's exposure would exceed the OSHA permissible exposure limit. (For example, if spending over two hours would result in unacceptably high dust levels, then four workers would be assigned to the job over an eight-hour shift.) This approach would not necessitate any changes in cleaning techniques, nor necessarily cause any loss of productivity. Workers could be reassigned to other tasks during the time intervals during which they no longer clean the product.

2. *Work practices:* Employees could use cleaning techniques that would reduce the generation of dust. Perhaps they need only to avoid shaking or jarring the product while cleaning it.

In the case of the workers suffering from back strain, an administrative control would be to assign helpers to workers who lift packages over a certain weight.

Administrative controls are less effective solutions to safety hazards than are engineering controls because they rely on the cooperation of the workers whom they protect. Ensuring that workers change their cleaning techniques to reduce dust generation, or seeing that they always get help before lifting a package over a certain weight, requires constant supervision, especially if these rules slow down productivity and are viewed by the worker as an impediment to productivity.

☐ PROTECTIVE EQUIPMENT

Protective equipment is the next weapon in the safety professional's arsenal against occupational health and safety hazards. Protective equipment, such as respirators, safety glasses, and specialized gloves, ranks a distant fourth as a response to safety hazards because proper use is difficult to enforce, and it often reduces both a worker's level of comfort and his or her ability to move and manipulate objects.

Wearing protective equipment requires two types of training. First, the employee needs to be able to identify situations where the equipment is necessary. This may be simple (always wearing safety glasses in the plant) or complex (selecting and donning the appropriate respirator for a given inhalation hazard). The second type of training required is motivational. The employee must be convinced that the protection offered by protective equipment is worth the level of discomfort it produces. Because we have a natural aversion to anything that reduces our comfort level or interferes with our ability to manipulate objects, the use of protective equipment in the workplace requires constant oversight and motivational training.

For some jobs, a variety of these techniques can be used. For example, an employee may be provided with a vacuum instead of an air hose to clean equipment (an engineering control), and that employee may also wear a respirator when performing the job in case the vacuum is not effective enough (use of protective equipment).

Determining what hazards can be addressed by engineering and administrative controls, and when employees can be protected by protective equipment, is an essential step in the process of establishing training goals. The goal of safety training professionals is to protect the health of the worker. They cannot do that until they know what the hazards are and how they are going to be addressed.

Any attempt to develop safety training prior to carefully considering whether some nontraining approach will be more effective will result in training that is unfocused. The training may have high production values, the instructors may be interesting, and the trainees may score appreciably higher on the posttests than they do on the pretests, but the training will probably not result in significant reductions in workplace accident rates.

 ## COMPLIANCE WITH THE LABORATORY STANDARD

In October 1992, OSHA issued regulation 1910.1450 (Occupational Exposure to Hazardous Chemicals in Laboratories), commonly called *the laboratory standard*. The laboratory standard required extensive training and monitoring of laboratory workers to ensure that their health was not jeopardized by the chemicals with which they worked. Like all OSHA standards, this one defined the employees covered by the laboratory standard (those to whom the regulations in the standard applied) in terms of their potential for exposure and their job responsibilities.

Many companies that employed chemists, laboratory technicians, and other personnel with responsibilities related to laboratory chemicals responded to the training provisions in the laboratory standard in what might seem like a logical manner. They made two lists: one of the training requirements in the laboratory standard and one of their own current training program for laboratory workers. They noted any areas where their training fell short of the requirements of the laboratory standard, and they revised their program so that it was at least as comprehensive as the one required by the OSHA standard. Because the laboratory standard addressed many health and safety issues besides training, the medical, personnel, and occupational safety departments at these companies presumably also compared their policies and programs to the new standard and made the necessary adjustments.

This approach to compliance with the new standard may or may not be the best one for any given company. To determine this, a company's department heads would have to look at every requirement in the laboratory standard, consider every possible option for meeting that requirement, and then select the most effective option. Only when training was identified as the best option would the training department begin to develop or revise programs.

Considering all the options may improve accuracy and productivity and lower the accident rate, as one company proved in responding to OSHA regulation 1910.1450 (see preceding discussion). This company assembled a committee to compare its present laboratory worker training to the training required by the OSHA standard, and that committee noted that the laboratory standard exempted workers if they used only chemical test kits because, in normal use, these kits resulted in no measurable exposures of employees to chemicals. The committee researched these kits and found that the kits could be used for much of the analysis performed at their company. They then performed a cost analysis and determined that the cost of using the kits (which resulted in many of the company's workers being exempted from the laboratory standard) was far lower than complying with all of the standard's provisions. Once the test kit program was in place the committee also discovered that, because employees found it easier to use the test kits than to perform conventional chemical analysis, the accuracy of the analysis had improved. Thus, the company accomplished the following:

- Improved worker safety by reducing the possibility of chemical exposure

- Decreased costs by exempting many employees from the requirements of the OSHA laboratory standard

- Improved the accuracy of their chemical analysis, which could lower injury rates and manufacturing costs and raise product quality

All these benefits stemmed from performing a needs analysis, that is, systematically determining the best possible solution to a safety problem instead of merely assuming training was the solution.

Of course, there will be occupational safety hazards for which training is part of the solution. Once the hazardous tasks have been identified from the job hazard analysis, and, where possible, those hazards are reduced by other means, a group of tasks will remain where safety training will be required. Those tasks should be categorized in several ways.

First, categorize the tasks by priority. By using the company's accident history and by discussing the tasks with workers and supervisors who perform them, determine which training tasks can be categorized as high, medium, and low according to their importance in being completed.

Second, categorize the tasks according to the domain or domains of learning in which the training will take place.

 ## DOMAINS OF LEARNING

There are three domains of learning (see Table 4.3):

1. *Cognitive:* Cognitive behaviors mainly require mental abilities, such as recollection, reasoning, and evaluation. Performing long division is a cognitive skill, as is inspecting a chemical factory or programming a computer. Common verbs used to describe behaviors in this domain are *analyze, assess, deduce, discuss,* or *calculate.* In all the above examples, a small amount of mind-body coordination is required, but the overwhelming demand on the worker is mental.

2. *Affective:* Values are in the affective domain. A value is an object or concept about which people care enough to take action. Common verbs used to describe learning activities in this domain are *accept, appreciate, respond, understand,* and *value.* The action may be to hold on to a value they already possess or obtain a value they do not yet own. Affirmative action training involves values, as does sexual harassment training. In both cases the values are fairness and social justice. Obviously, safety training has a strong affective component. Workers must value their health enough to behave in ways that reduce risks. Considering

TABLE 4.3 Domains of Learning

Cognitive	Affective	Psychomotor
(Mental or intellectual) analyze, assess, deduce, discuss, or calculate	*(Feelings or values)* accept, appreciate, respond, understand, and value	*(Mind-body coordination)* arrange, assemble, overhaul, simulate, and utilize

that health is a universal value, cutting across ethnic, national, and cultural lines, one would assume that safety would be an "easy sell." The statistics indicate otherwise. Often, convenience or speed is valued more highly than health. Or possibly the risk of loss of health is perceived as low in a particular situation, and the value of speed or convenience is considered high.

3. *Psychomotor:* The psychomotor domain includes behaviors that require mind-body coordination, such as adjusting a carburetor, operating a lathe, or playing basketball. Common actions used in describing learning activities within this domain are *arrange, assemble, overhaul, simulate,* and *utilize.* Include any "hands-on" activities within this domain.

All safety training will fall into at least one of these domains. The domains in which the learning will take place will determine a great deal about how the training is designed and implemented. The facilities needed for affective and psychomotor training are likely to be quite different. Affective training requires classrooms and typical classroom support (blackboards, flips charts, VCRs, and monitors, and so forth); psychomotor training requires a workshop with equipment that resembles the operations in which the trainee will actually engage. This could range from an auto shop with engine parts for a vocational automotive student to an operating room with cadavers for a medical intern. Consequently, training developers cannot begin to plan training until they determine the domains of learning in which the training falls.

The best method for determining the proper domain of learning is to go back to the experts, the people doing the work. Domains of learning are fundamental concepts; they can be easily conveyed to workers with even a basic education. Those workers can then review the tasks on the job hazard analysis for which training has been deemed necessary and identify the proper domain of learning.

A couple of examples may help illustrate this.

Workers have identified grinding parts as a task that is hazardous to the eyes. The grinding wheel already has a shield (an engineering control), and workers are required to wear goggles and a face shield (protective equipment). In what domain would the safety training for this task be? There would be cognitive tasks, such as determining which materials could be ground with which grinding wheel, inspecting the wheels for defects, and knowing the correct wheel speed if the grinder is adjustable. There would also be psychomotor tasks, such as using the correct pressure on the work piece during the grinding operation and changing wheels if needed. The affective domain would include valuing one's eyesight enough to perform the inspection and use the protective equipment. This particular task would involve all three domains.

Contrast this to the task of monitoring a process control panel at a chemical manufacturing plant. This would have a negligible psychomotor component: the skill required to flip switches and turn dials would not require training. However, the job would have an extremely high cognitive component—interpreting the data presented by the instrumentation on the panel, assessing and evaluating possible responses to the data, and deciding on a course of action. Because the operator may occasionally need to weigh the conflicting demands of safety and productivity and determine acceptable risk levels, this work would also fall in the affective domain.

1. List five groups that should participate in the process of reviewing a completed job hazard analysis and recommending remedial actions.

2. List three approaches, in addition to training, that should be considered when correcting hazards identified by a job hazard analysis.

3. List three reasons training is often not the most effective method of correcting a safety hazard.

4. What are the benefits of correcting a safety hazard through engineering controls?

5. Differentiate between an engineering control and an administrative control.

Perfect Paint Company paints consumer items and applies industrial coatings to industrial equipment. One of the spray booth operators is complaining of a hoarse voice and sore throat. He believes the problem is related to the solvents in the paint, and the possibility is confirmed by the site industrial hygienist.

6. Describe an engineering control that may reduce the hazard. Include one advantage and one disadvantage to this approach.

7. Describe an administrative control that may reduce the hazard. Include one advantage and one disadvantage to this approach.

8. *a.* Describe the role safety training would play in question 6.
   b. Describe the role safety training would play in question 7.

9. List two disadvantages of relying on protective equipment to alleviate a safety hazard.

10. Identify a safety or health hazard at your firm for which training in the affective domain is required.

▓ REFERENCES

1. Gloria Regalbuto, "Targeting the Bottom Line," *Training & Development* (April 1992):30.

2. Code of Federal Regulations, 29 CFR 1910.134, Respiratory Protection.

IDENTIFYING GOALS AND OBJECTIVES

KEY CONCEPTS OF CHAPTER FIVE

Effective training requires clearly stated, measurable goals and objectives.

A training goal is a general statement of how the training will support the company's mission, performance, or product.

A learning objective is a description of what the trainees will be able to do as a result of the training, the conditions under which they will be able to perform, and the quality of their work.

Once the content of training has been determined, the next step in developing a training program is to describe what the end result of training will be—that is, what skills, knowledge, and attitudes trainees will acquire if they successfully complete the program. The program will be based on the hazards identified in the job hazard analysis. The training will address the skills and abilities the trainees will need to use the engineering controls, administrative controls, and protective equipment necessary to mitigate or eliminate those hazards.

The intended result of training is stated in the form of *training goals* and *learning objectives*. These are both statements of the intent of the instruction. They differ in their specificity and breadth.

Training goals are general statements of the overall goals of the training program. They are logically derived from the mission statement of the company, if it has one, and the mission statements of both the safety and training departments. The training goals provide both the focus and the overall direction of the program. They describe the overall effect that the training program, if it is successful, will have on the company. For example, the goal of a company's hazard communication program may be:

> *Provide the employees with the knowledge and skills*
> *necessary to obtain and properly interpret any*
> *information related to the safety and health risks of the*
> *materials to which they are exposed on the job.*

Note that the goal does not state how this will be accomplished, nor does it state the specific skills and behaviors the trainees will demonstrate on the job. Those are both important bits of information, but they are not addressed in the goal. However, a training goal may include some other constraints, such as budget and time. This would depend on:

- To whom the goal will be communicated, and

- Whether it will be used as part of an evaluation of the training or safety department, or of any of the personnel in those departments.

Other management personnel in a supervisory relationship with the training developers will probably be very interested in time and budget commitments. Management personnel not in this position will not, nor will trainees.

For the former group, the goal could be expanded to state:

By September 13, 1993, at a capital cost not exceeding $20,000, and using not more than 800 worker hours, provide the employees with the knowledge and skills necessary to obtain and properly interpret any information related to the safety and health risks of the materials to which they are exposed on the job.

If safety training is to be comprehensive, these training goals should encompass all the performance-related deficiencies identified by the job hazard analysis.

Once the training goals are developed, the training-related hazards should be grouped under them. One or more learning objectives should be written to cover each hazard. A learning objective is a specific statement of an observable behavior that the trainees will demonstrate if they successfully complete the training.

Although each learning objective does not begin with "The trainee will be able to," that statement is implied in each learning objective. The objective describes what the trainee will be able to do in terms of (1) the behavior the trainee will be able to demonstrate, (2) the conditions under which the behavior will take place, and (3) the standard or quality of that behavior.

When writing objectives, the most common mistakes are focusing on either what the instructor will discuss in class or what the trainee will perform as a learning exercise. Neither of these activities should be described in an objective. Because writers of objectives frequently have difficulty differentiating among components that do and do not belong in an objective, we will consider some poorly written and well-written objectives, and determine what qualities place them in either category. The following is a poorly written objective:

The trainee will read a chapter of the assigned text each week and will answer all the even-numbered questions at the back of the chapter with 90 percent accuracy.

This is a good example of a homework assignment, but it is a wretched objective because the final interest of the employer whom the training department represents is never in how well the trainee answers questions in the back of the book. That is not why management allocated a safety training budget. The mind-set that leads a training supervisor to describe the outcome of training in this fashion also results in training programs that lack a clear and obvious connection to organizational or departmental goals. Employees at all levels of authority should find it easy to identify a causal relationship between safety training and the reduction of occupational injuries. If this relationship is unclear at the beginning of training (because of poorly written objectives) or compromised during the course of training, training personnel should expect to be engaged in a continuous and probably losing battle to obtain adequate funding and staffing, and to have employees released from regular assignments for training.

To correct this objective, consider why it would benefit the company for the trainee to read those chapters. How was reading those chapters intended to affect the trainee's on-the-job behavior? Presumably some skill was identified in the job hazard analysis as being important to the trainee's safety. For example, the trainee oversees the production of floor wax. She must periodically perform some analytical work at a quality-control station, and the analysis involves chemicals. Some of these chemicals are incompatible, and the trainee needs to know which ones should not be mixed. The text referred to in the above objective was on chemistry, and the chapter was on incompatible chemicals. Now we are getting somewhere. The objective should have read:

> *The trainee will identify all combinations of chemicals available at quality-control station 4 that are incompatible, discuss at least one reason for the incompatibility, and state the possible adverse health effects of mixing the chemicals.*

A second objective related to the same job responsibility might be:

> *For each possible mixture of incompatible chemicals at quality-control station 4, the trainees will demonstrate a response that will protect them and their co-workers from injury.*

Now that two properly written objectives have been presented, we

TABLE 5.1   Components of Objectives

Performance	Condition	Standard
States *what* the trainee will be albe to do (e.g., the trainee will perform adult CPR).	States *under what circumstances* the trainee will be able to do it (e.g., on a mannequin, with no prompting).	Provides *measures of quality,* such as speed and accuracy (e.g., according to American Red Cross guidelines).

will consider the three components (performance, conditions, and standards) that make up a properly written learning objective (see Table 5.1).

COMPONENTS OF EFFECTIVE OBJECTIVES

PERFORMANCE

The performance is the statement of what the trainee will do. It should include an action verb that describes observable and measurable behavior. *Appreciate, understand,* and *know* are all action verbs that are not measurable and should not be used for training. They may, however, imply important knowledge or skills needed to perform a job properly. On the other hand, *select, manipulate, discriminate,* and *identify* are all verbs that clearly denote specific actions. If the objective writers carefully consider what behaviors were included in the first group of action verbs, they will be able to describe those behaviors in observable verbs like those in the second group.

Some measurable performances are:

List the necessary steps in responding to a hazardous chemical spill.

Fill out a manifest form for a shipment of asbestos waste that is being taken to a landfill.

Select the proper tools needed to disassemble a sump pump.

Lubricate a 1991 Chevrolet Corvette.

CONDITIONS

Jack Training checks his voice mail. There is a curt message from Jane Plant Manager: "Stop in my office as soon as possible." She doesn't sound happy. He reports to her office, and her secretary gives him a look that can only be interpreted as "Pick up a newspaper on your way home and play close attention to the 'help wanted' classifieds."

As Jack sits across from her desk, Jane glares at him and asks, "How many welders were enrolled in that MIG welding class held last year?"

"Seventeen of them—the whole crew."

"And how many of them passed?"

"They all did."

"We started work on the steam generator repair yesterday. There were five accidents: three burns and two electric shocks. That means in one day we doubled our incidence of recordable accidents for the year. One of those burns was a third-degree burn to the right hand. I also received a report from the quality-control department. There was a 70 percent failure rate on the welds. The welders are grinding out the bad welds now. I am paying contractors to come in and reweld when they are finished. The production line will be down three additional days. I haven't figured out yet how much over budget the job is going to be."

Being a good training supervisor, Jack did not assume that either the accidents or the defective welds were due to training. He began to review mentally the other reasons the welds might be unsatisfactory: equipment failures, wrong weld rods, workers being rushed, and so on. Being a good plant manager, Jane knew exactly what Jack was thinking and broke in before he could reply.

"This was a performance problem, Jack, so don't think about blaming the materials. The quality-control people say the equipment and supplies are right for the job. The shift supervisor said the men are trying, but they don't know what they are doing. Got that, Jack? *They don't know what they are doing.*"

Jack's vacation was starting tomorrow, and he had already purchased plane tickets. But in the new mean, lean, quality-oriented, customer-driven, downsized world of U.S. manufacturing, you don't tell your boss about vacations and plane tickets when the production line is down.

Poor Jack. He pushed hard for this training program. He was convinced that company personnel could do the welding just as well as vendors and much more economically. The training was carefully planned, and the trainees were thoroughly tested. Where did he go wrong? Jack did not take into account the conditions under which the actual work would be performed. The training took place in a welding lab. It was clean and well ventilated. The trainees were comfortable and were guided by excellent instructors.

The production welding took place inside a natural-gas-to-water heat exchanger. The welders were uncomfortable as they worked in cramped, confined spaces and had to wear respirators. What's more, the brand of welding equipment they used on the job was different from that they used in training. It was selected by the purchasing department because it was the least expensive equipment that met all the bid specifications. The workers perceived it as being inferior to the training equipment, and there was widespread talk among them that they were being asked to perform new and difficult work with inadequate equipment. Finally, both the weld rods and the tubes being welded, although right for the job, were different from those used in training, and they had different melting and burning characteristics.

To ensure effective training that produces a safe, competent worker, the conditions of the work must be taken into account. This is not to say that the conditions of the training must be exactly the same as the conditions on the job. This is often not feasible (although some very sophisticated simulators used for training nuclear power control room operators and passenger jet pilots come very close to exact reproductions of on-the-job conditions). A thorough job hazard analysis of the welding work would have revealed that the work was to be done in a confined space, for example. Then the appropriate combination of engineering controls, administrative controls, protective equipment, and safety training could have been planned to minimize the hazards confined spaces can cause. Also, once a brand of welding equipment was selected, the salesperson could have come in, very likely at no charge, and conducted a brief orientation session of the special features of that brand. The training could have included some subtle sales work, so that the workers could have been persuaded of the value of the equipment they were using.

These considerations are critical to safety. A trainee may well be able to perform a job adequately in a classroom or laboratory, but not be able to do so on the job because of distractions or other circumstances that were not present in the classroom. For example, a trainee may be able to clean a respirator in class, but will he or she clean it properly when it is contaminated with toxic chemicals? Will a trainee be able to discern between a respirator that can be cleaned and one that should be discarded because it cannot be properly sanitized?

Let us now rewrite the previously presented objectives so that appropriate conditions are included. Like the performances, the conditions should be derived from the job hazard analysis.

Given copies of the Department of Transportation's *Guide to Hazardous Chemicals,* the appropriate Material Safety Data Sheets, and a computer loaded with emergency response software, list the necessary steps in responding to a given hazardous chemical spill.

Given the necessary data and a copy of the appropriate EPA regulations, fill out a manifest form for a shipment of asbestos waste that is being taken to a landfill.

Given the manufacturer's specifications manual, select the proper tools needed to disassemble a sump pump.

Given the necessary tools and supplies, lubricate a 1991 Chevrolet Corvette for operation in cold weather.

The word *given* does not always need to be included in the conditions of an objective, but the idea implied by *given,* that special factors that affect the performance are being described, is always present in the condition.

☐ STANDARDS

One of the bywords of American business today is *quality,* and it's a good thing Americans are talking and thinking about it. However quality is measured—freedom from defects, durability, user-oriented design—more and more firms, American and non-American, are offering it in the workplace. What used to be the Japanese challenge, for example, is now the Asian Rim challenge. And the free-market zone that has already emerged in North and South America, and that may be emerging in

Europe, will be an additional source of competition for quality-oriented markets. The United States has already risen to the quality challenge in many ways, and by incorporating standards into objectives, those developing safety training programs can be part of America's quality effort.

Each objective written can include a standard of quality for the performance that is described. That standard can be described in conventional quality terms, such as absence of error or adherence to an accepted quality norm. Some standards for objectives are "with 90 percent accuracy," "within 10/1000's of an inch," or "at a rate of 13 per hour."

Let's take one final look at our example objectives, this time adding standards to the performances and conditions already written.

Given copies of the Department of Transportation's *Guide to Hazardous Chemicals,* the appropriate Material Safety Data Sheets, and a computer loaded with emergency response software, list the necessary steps in responding to a hazardous chemical spill with 100 percent accuracy (standard of accuracy added).

Given the necessary data and a copy of the appropriate EPA regulations, completely fill out a manifest form for a shipment of asbestos waste that is being taken to a landfill within 30 minutes (standard of speed added).

Given the manufacturer's specifications, select the proper tools needed to disassemble a sump pump. No necessary tools must be omitted, and only one unnecessary tool may be included (standard of selection accuracy added).

Given the necessary tools and supplies and a selection of lubricants, lubricate, within one hour, a 1991 Chevrolet Corvette with the proper chassis and engine lubricants for operation in cold weather (standard of speed added).

As with the performance, the standard must be matched carefully to the level of behavior identified in the job hazard analysis. Lists of objectives are available, grouped at various levels of performance, for each of the learning domains.

A properly written objective is a thing of beauty; like a fine poem, the selection and placement of every word is carefully thought out.

"But," thinks the reader, "I'm not being paid to write poetry." But, responds the author, a well-written objective is also a thing of financial beauty. It should warm the heart of the flintiest company accountant because well-written objectives permit training personnel to make difficult decisions related to the duration and content of training, and duration and content relate directly to cost.

The following questions can be answered by carefully examining the objectives and comparing them with the course content:

Does this video need to included in the hazard communication training?

Can the safety audit training be completed in 90 minutes instead of an hour?

Does the hand tool safety program need a hands–on session, or can it be presented entirely in the classroom?

Can we condense our regulatory training without compromising the quality?

If clearly written objectives are not available, it is impossible to answer these questions in a manner that will provide the training supervisor with any confidence that decisions regarding course content can be defended to other parties within the company (such as cost accountants or safety personnel) or outside of the company (such as OSHA compliance officers or insurance auditors).

One company cuts down on the costs of OSHA- and EPA-required training by alternating full-length and condensed versions of the training programs. The full-length versions include lectures, videos, and motivational materials. The condensed versions are brief written reviews of information that is either required by one of these agencies or deemed critical by the company's training personnel.

Trainees have indicated on evaluations that they like this approach; it helps prevent the training from becoming tedious. Supervisors like it because it makes the scheduling of training more manageable. But the important point is that it was possible for this company to simultaneously condense and maintain the integrity of the training because the instructors could check training content against clearly written objectives.

Having determined what sections of the job hazard analysis need to be addressed by training, and then describing the purpose of that training in observable, measurable terms, the safety training developers now have a solid foundation and can confidently move on to the next step in the development process—developing the learning activities.

1. Write one training goal for your company.

2. If your company has a mission statement, explain how the above goal ties into the mission statement.

3. For the goal stated in question 2, write one cognitive learning objective including:
  a. A statement of performance
  b. Conditions under which the performance must occur
  c. A standard of quality for the performance

4. Safety training objectives should be derived from which of the following?
  a. The job hazard analysis
  b. The test of the written materials used for training
  c. The lesson plan
  d. The test questions

5. List two action verbs that describe measurable performances in the:
  a. Cognitive domain.
  b. Affective domain.
  c. Psychomotor domain.

6. Write one objective in the affective (values) domain.

7. Write a safety training goal, the accomplishment of which will require meeting objectives in all three learning domains.

8. *a.* State one training situation at your company where the conditions of training are quite different from the conditions on the job.
  b. What are some steps that can be taken to make that training better resemble the work?

DEVELOPING LEARNING ACTIVITIES

KEY CONCEPTS OF CHAPTER SIX

Once the learning objectives are written, the trainer must determine the best methods for conveying that information to the trainees. That determination necessitates considering any characteristics of the trainees that affect the way they learn.

Once both the learning objectives and the learning characteristics of the trainees are known, training materials can be selected or developed that are consistent with both.

Training experiences and materials (lectures, tests, videos, discussions, hands-on sessions, and so on) must be structured (set in the proper order in relation to the learner and to each other) to maximize the effectiveness of the learning experience.

Any fool can present a training program.

Somewhere out there in Safety Training Land is a "canned" (pre-developed) training program that likely covers the topics that have been identified as learning needs during the job hazard analysis. In addition to the canned programs, there are firms that specialize in training program development. Finding the canned program, or the vendor, may require work, possibly even much work, but it requires little creative thinking. It is simply a matter of persistence and negotiation.

Fools cannot, however, change the behaviors of their co-workers so that the co-workers are safer and healthier. Making that type of impact requires wisdom, insight, and creativity. Trainees have a remarkable ability to enter and exit a training program unaffected, with absolutely no change in their workplace behavior to indicate that they went through the training. This is true even when the trainees pass a test on the material on which they were trained. The author would love to quote a statistic on how many training dollars in a given year were wasted because they did not result in the desired changes in on-the-job behaviors, but in many cases there is no procedure in place for measuring whether training transferred over to the workplace. Management simply does not know whether the money devoted to training was well spent.

This problem—determining if the training made any difference in behavior—is most easily resolved when personnel are trained in technical skills that are essential to performing their job properly. If they can do their job, the training was successful. The problem is most difficult when the training is meant to affect the quality of their work, and the skill taught is one of many factors that contribute to quality (for example, training a supervisor in verbal communications).

Ultimately, the question of whether training had the desired impact is answered during the evaluation of the trainees, but the developers, while selecting or developing learning activities, should be asking themselves, "How will completion of this activity move the trainees toward the behaviors identified in the objectives?" Following these three steps will ensure that learning activities succeed in enabling most trainees to master the behaviors described in the objectives:

1. Identify the learning characteristics of the target population.

2. Develop or select instructional materials and activities.

3. Structure the materials and activities into the training program.

IDENTIFYING LEARNING CHARACTERISTICS OF THE TARGET POPULATION

If we hope to change the behaviors of the trainees, it helps to know them intimately. What motivates them to work? A need for money? Pride in what they produce? A need for structure? Enjoyment of being part of a team? What do they see as their primary role? Providing for their family? Earning money to get through school? Being able to travel on vacation? Would they choose more vacation time or more pay if they were given the choice? How much initiative will they take in learning? How much structure are they comfortable with? How much learning time will pass before they get bored? What size should the learning units be? Too little information at one time will make for a tedious training session; too much will be intellectually indigestible, and the trainees will stop paying attention. How much can they absorb before they are mentally fatigued? If they are confronted with a problem in front of the class, will they rise to the challenge or will they be embarrassed?

These are all important questions that affect learning speed and scope. They also determine whether the skills and attitudes acquired during the training will transfer to the job. None of these things can be determined by identifying what skills require training; they can be determined only by analyzing the trainees themselves. That is what is meant by "determining the target population"—gathering information about the trainees that allows the training developers to present the training in a fashion that:

- Holds the trainees' attention

- Allows the trainees to learn

- Encourages the trainees to demonstrate their new skills on the job

In *Developing Vocational Instruction* Mager and Beach state, "It is foolish and wasteful to design a course without defining the target population. The major characteristics of the target population constitute the starting point of the course."[1]

The trainees are a target. Training personnel are aiming certain behavior changes at them that will reduce the possibility that they are injured on the job. Scoring a bull's-eye entails having the trainees demonstrate those behavior changes in class, during their evaluation, and on the job. To be perfectly accurate, it is not the safety trainer's responsibility to ensure that safe behavior is demonstrated on the job; that is the responsibility of line management and of the trainees themselves. It is, however, the the safety trainer's responsibility to ensure that the trainees are capable of performing the skills for which they were trained and are predisposed toward using those skills on the job. The second part, ensuring that the trainees are predisposed toward demonstrating the skills, is as important as the first, and it is much more difficult to accomplish and determine.

"Most loss control programs have difficulty in effectively addressing the intangible aspects of the employee-machine interaction. Those items that affect the employee's decision-making process, effective training, safety motivation, physical and mental stresses, are secondary to machine refinement. The physical aspects of the man-machine system are more objectively correlated, *while the elements of the behavioral sciences—the reasons why employees make or fail to make safety decisions—are more subjective and have not yet been widely accepted in the industrial setting*"[2] (italics added).

With that in mind, let us look at the characteristics of the target population and how they affect the way safety training is developed and presented. Mager and Beach list the following characteristics of the target population that may affect learning: physical characteristics, education, motivation, interests, and, as a single group, attitudes, biases, and prejudices.[3] (see Table 6.1). We will consider the role of each.

☐ PHYSICAL CHARACTERISTICS

Depending on the physical demands of the job, physical characteristics may play quite a large role in the training or no role at all. The safety trainer must ensure that the relationship between the physical demands of the training and the physical abilities of the trainees is accounted for when planning training. It is bad enough when an employee is hurt on the job. When an employee is hurt during training, particularly during safety training, the credibility of the instructor, and of the entire training department, is undermined. Another important consideration is that the trainee be physically qualified to perform the work on the job, which

TABLE 6.1   The Target Population

Physical Characteristics	Education	Motivation	Interests	Attitudes, Biases, Prejudices
Strength, weight, endurance	Prior training related to specific skills Academic background	How completing training will affect pay, promotions, self-esteem, prestige	Relationship of training to nonoccupational areas (hobbies, associations, etc.)	Preconceptions with which the trainees will enter that may affect learning

may well be a far more strenuous endeavor than performing the work during training.

The work may be far more strenuous on the job because of the speed at which the work must be completed, or, more likely, because of the difference between the work environment and the training environment. The most obvious physical demand of the job is moving heavy objects, but a number of other requirements should be considered, including dexterity, flexibility, speed, and ability to withstand heat and cold stress and temperature extremes.

Decisions regarding the ability of the worker to perform the work must be made in context with the provisions of the Americans with Disabilities Act. Employers have a legal responsibility to make reasonable accommodations in the workplace for employees who are physically disabled. To protect themselves from liability, employers should be prepared to defend any decisions as to why the workplace cannot be modified to accommodate a worker with physical limitations.

There are other considerations besides the legal and ethical ones related to fairness in the workplace for the physically disabled. The fact that a job requires special physical qualities should immediately raise a "red flag" to management as far as that job's hazard potential. Also, because only a limited number of people will be available for jobs that demand special physical qualifications, supervisors will be limited when they are scheduling personnel to fill all the positions on a shift. These are a few good reasons to try and "engineer out" the special demands of the job. This may be possible by providing special machinery for lifting heavy items or reaching distant ones.

There will, however, be positions for which this is impossible. When special physical qualifications are required for performing the job, those requirements should be clearly stated prerequisites for receiving the training. Training employees to perform some specific work will obviously give them the impression that they can also do the work in the workplace. It will be demoralizing to employees if, after they pass the training, they are informed that they are not qualified to perform the work for some nontraining-related reason. It will also be an example of weak management.

Establishing the physical qualifications for the job is not a training responsibility. These qualifications should be determined and enforced by line management or the personnel department.

☐ EDUCATION

The education level of the trainees will have a significant effect on both the content and the structure of the training program. Education's effect on content will be easier to deal with. A well-designed training program does not cover information that the trainees already know. The best way to determine what the trainee already knows is a pretest, but a familiarity with target populations' educational history can provide the safety trainer with some solid working assumptions. For example, if all the trainees enrolled in an electrical safety program are degreed electrical engineers, the trainer can assume they are already familiar with basic electrical terms (voltage, amperage, and so on), and no training time is needed for those concepts.

Education level also affects structure. If trainees are unfamiliar with a subject, they are also likely to be uncomfortable with it. They will learn best in a carefully structured course with regular and fairly close evaluation intervals and frequent summaries. The initial evaluations should be easy enough so that a trainee can experience a string of successes that will positively affect his or her attitude toward the job. Trainees who are comfortable with the subject would find this type of training tedious. They would be much more open to a self-paced training program that also provides for self-discovery.

An example might prove helpful. Consider the following training goal: training workers to rebuild a specific motor. The target population falls into two distinct groups: Group 1 consists of skilled electricians who rebuild other motors but are not familiar with this particular one; Group 2 consists of new employees without any electrical background.

Group 1 may not need any more training and can be left in a room with the motor, the training manual, and the necessary tools. Make it clear to the trainees that they will be evaluated, and that work performed in an unsafe manner will be considered just as wrong as work that is technically incorrect. Group 2 would need a carefully structured program where both concept and application are systematically developed and reinforced, starting with the fundamentals of electricity and moving on to the basic types of motors. A creative safety trainer who must deal with both groups may well use Group 1 to train Group 2.

☐ MOTIVATION

Motivation is a key component in any learning process, and it is one aspect of the target population with which training development personnel must be thoroughly familiar prior to developing any training. Will the target population be motivated to change their behavior? This should have been determined while establishing the need for training, because the most important question about motivation is "Is this training addressing a learning-related problem?" Presumably, at this point the instructor is confident that at least a component of the problem is learning related.

Unless trainees are motivated to learn, they will not do so. The person presenting the training, be it the developer or the instructor, must know what motivates the trainees. Will they be able to work more safely after completing the training? Are they the type of people likely to appreciate that? Is successful completion of the training necessary to maintain or improve the trainees' job status? The latter is probably the most common motivator for job training. The instructor thus has an excellent motivator to ensure that the trainees will work hard to learn the skills needed to complete the class successfully, though the trainees will not necessarily carry those skills back to the workplace. It is also likely that trainees will experience a great deal of anxiety if they are having difficulty with the material. The trainer should think about how to keep them relaxed.

Eliciting safe behavior on the job may require an entirely different set of motivators. Are the trainees likely to find the material interesting? Will completing the training improve their security, stature, or sense of self-worth? Whatever the reason, the trainer should have a list of motivators for the particular group to be instructed, and he or she should appeal to those motivators during the class. If the trainer cannot think of any motivators, the training session may not be successful and will probably be frustrating.

☐ INTERESTS

Just as the learning process requires that the trainees begin with something they already know and move on to that which they do not, motivating the trainees to pay attention and to carry the new skills back to the workplace requires that the training be related to something that the trainees are already interested in. That relationship should be continually reinforced throughout the training. If that is accomplished, we can be reasonably sure that the trainees will leave the workplace predisposed toward using their new skills in the workplace.

How does one determine the interests of the trainees? How about asking them? Completing a survey of interests may be helpful. Making good use of lunches and breaks can provide the instructor with invaluable information about what interests the trainees. (Effective instructors do not go on "break" during breaks; they listen carefully to comments about the class and work at winning over the skeptics.) Comments that trainees make in class also provide information. One CPR instructor was faced with a loss of interest in CPR training because of the AIDS crisis. People were afraid of acquiring HIV from the CPR mannequin. AIDS training helped correct the problem. The trainees knew, at least intellectually, that a properly cleaned CPR mannequin was *not* a mode of transmission for any disease, including AIDS. But the number of employees willing to perform CPR on a mannequin was still lower than it had been. The instructor determined, through informal conversations, that most trainees thought of performing CPR in terms of rescuing family members. The instructor then began emphasizing, at the beginning of the class, that these skills could be used at home and that it was more likely that the CPR would be used on a loved one than on a co-worker (who may or may not be a loved one).

Because the trainees were interested in the well-being of their families, that motivational technique provided the impetus to restore the attendance in CPR training. The safety trainer has an inherent advantage when it comes to appealing to the interests of the trainees: whereas only some people are interested in performing their job well, nearly everyone is interested in avoiding pain and illness. One technique for gaining the trainees' interests is to solicit anecdotes from the group about their personal experiences with occupational safety and health hazards.

"Jane, tell us about your experience with carpal tunnel syndrome. Did you lose full use of your wrist? Joe, exactly what happened when you lost your balance and hurt your back? If you were in the same situation again, what would you do differently?"

☐ ATTITUDES

Trainees do not enter the training environment as "tabulae rasae" —intellectual blank slates. They have attitudes and biases, some work related and some social. How do they feel about the company in general? Was their last experience with training positive or negative? What attitudes do they already hold about the subject on which they are being trained? Is it important or unimportant? Interesting or boring? Do they think they already know more than the trainer?

Sexual and racial biases may also affect the attitude toward learning. A group of male welders, coming from an all-male maintenance department, might be biased against a female instructor. Trainees may be biased against an instructor from a different ethnic group than their own. These kinds of problems are minimized when a company actively promotes mutual respect and equal opportunity, instead of merely responding to problems after they arise.

The safety trainer cannot always change the attitudes of the trainees. Obviously, in cases like those described in the above paragraph, it would not be ethical to even accommodate the attitudes. But in the world of industrial training, ignorance is never bliss. There is always benefit to knowing all the factors that may affect learning in a given situation.

Determining the values of the target population is critical. If the instructor goes into the class without this knowledge, he or she must somehow establish it at the beginning, even if it is through informal conversation with the trainees. While this is a wholly unsatisfactory substitute for a systematic analysis of the target population, it is still far better than doing nothing to get to know the class.

Developing or Selecting Instructional Materials

Having identified the learning characteristics of the trainees, the safety program developer is now ready to either select or develop the instructional materials necessary to present the training program.

By this time many hours of hard work have already been invested in the training. Yet in many cases, this is the step in the development process with which they begin. Someone at a higher level of supervision has identified a problem and decided, often without considering options, that the solution to the problem is safety training. The person notifies the training supervisor that a training program is needed, and the training supervisor responds by selecting instructional materials (books, training manuals, videotapes, and so on) and implementing a training program. The process never includes instructors asking themselves or their co-workers whether the problem they are trying to solve could be handled by modifying equipment or changing procedures. The people doing the work are not asked how the hazard could be best minimized or eliminated. Little or nothing is known about the learning characteristics of the trainees, and the instructional materials are not previewed with the people doing the job.

A tremendous amount of corporate wealth—money, time, and talent—is wasted in this fashion. Employees still suffer accidents and occupational illnesses, which are even more tragic because the company had committed time and money to safety training. But the accidents still occur because their underlying cause was never identified and eliminated.

Thankfully, this will not happen at a company where instructional development guidelines are followed in developing safety training. The safety instructor who has gone through the steps described here will now be ready to confidently select training materials that will address real-world hazards by making measurable improvement in workers' safety-related behaviors.

The range of materials available for development has increased dramatically in the past decade, as has the available technology, so that instructors can develop professional-quality materials in-house. Using existing computer equipment, instructors can utilize user-friendly graphics programs to make charts, graphs, slides, and handouts that would have cost tens of thousands of dollars in the 1960s. While the equipment needed to do this is far from cheap, much of it, such as the computers, monitors, and printers, is probably already available. The only additional cost may be for the proper software.

One of the most obvious and most important rules to follow in selecting or developing materials is to match the training materials to the domain of learning. Fortunately, if the objectives that were developed earlier are reviewed carefully, and if the training materials are selected to match those objectives, the training will definitely match the domain of learning. Any behavior that contains words implying physical demonstrations (*manipulate, form, assemble, repair,* and so on) will require a hands-on learning environment. This invariably requires more space, time, and expense than training in the cognitive or psychomotor domain. It also presents one of the greatest temptations for training developers and instructors. Hands-on training sessions tend to decline into classroom training sessions—almost as if there were some physical law acting on them to transmute the former into the latter. Hands-on training often requires tedious, repetitious preparation before the training session and extensive clean up afterwards. It also often requires expensive equipment and is more difficult to modularize than classroom training. Often classroom training can be set up to be available on short notice, so if a certain work group is freed up, they can go into training. It is much more difficult to initiate hands-on training at the spur of the moment.

Be aware that the temptation exists to switch from hands-on training to classroom training. Make sure that you, or the instructors you oversee, are not trying to teach the trainees welding safety by having them watch a videotape or read a book. The video or book may be quite helpful before the hands-on session, to prepare the trainees for what they should pay attention to, or after the hands-on session, to reinforce the important principles they have learned. But cognitive mode training can never be adequate for teaching psychomotor skills.

The same applies to cognitive and affective behaviors, but they are less likely to translated into the wrong types of training.

☐ DEVELOPING AN IN-HOUSE TRAINING PROGRAM

While a review of the objectives should be adequate to determine what type of training is necessary to impart a particular skill to the trainees, it does not help the developer make one other important decision: whether to develop the training program in-house, pay a vendor to develop it, or select some "canned" (predeveloped) program. A critical determination to be made at this point is whether it is feasible, in terms of equipment and talent, to develop the training materials on-site.

The training supervisor must determine if anyone at the site has the skills to develop the training and whether the necessary equipment is available. Say, for example, that a decision has been made to develop a training program on welding safety. The program will include a videotape session, followed by hands-on training and evaluation, followed by a brief summary and a written test presented by a live instructor.

Before the question of the cost of developing the program in-house is even considered, someone must determine whether persons are available who have the skills required to:

- Write the videotape script, including the lesson plan for the live instructor portion and the hands-on demonstration

- Photograph, direct, and edit the videotape

- Instruct the hands-on and classroom sessions

It also must be determined whether budget money is available to purchase or rent:

- The necessary welding equipment

- The facilities needed to house the welding equipment, including adequate room, ventilation, electrical power, and lighting

- The video camera

- Production lighting

- Editing equipment

- Classroom space

Unless these skills and this much equipment are already available, or can be obtained, one should not consider developing the welding safety training program in-house. One of the most frustrating and unrewarding endeavors that a trainer can experience is to obtain a home quality video camera and attempt to develop training programs with it.

After a hard look at the cost and time involved in assembling all the components required for developing the training, the next option to be considered is hiring someone outside the company to present the training. There are a number of alternatives within this option: maintenance training companies will come out to a site and use that site's facilities. Some have trailers and bring all their equipment along, so that the only facilities the company needs to provide are space and an electrical hook-up. Many junior colleges and trade schools provide hands-on training to industry as well as to the community (at a higher price), and they are willing to customize programs to meet specific training needs. There are also firms that specialize in making training videos. Most will come out to a customer's site and make a video, or they may have welding safety video in stock that includes the necessary information.

The decision to buy a canned program, to develop one in-house, or to pay a contractor to develop a program is basically a cost-benefit question. The safety instructor should not proceed without performing a cost-benefit analysis.

☐ TAILORING PREDEVELOPED PROGRAMS TO MEET THE COMPANY'S NEEDS

It is unrealistic to expect any predeveloped program to meet the training needs that were identified by any given company's job hazard analysis. Too many hazards are specific to particular procedures. One of the critical responsibilities of a safety instructor is to ensure that the predeveloped program is properly tailored, that is, that the content of the program and the format meet the objectives determined during the task analysis and accommodate the learning style of the trainees.

Consider again the welding safety program. Assume that the safety instructor has established, through a cost-benefit analysis, that the most economical way to present the training would be to use a vendor who comes to the site in a trailer and presents a predeveloped program. Site training personnel responsible for welding safety should:

- Meet with the vendor and review the learning objectives, checking the objectives carefully against the previously prepared material. It is essential that the company training personnel ensure that the necessary changes are in the lesson plan. One of the most effective (though tedious) ways of accomplishing this is to organize the learning objectives into groups and assign each objective a code number. Then match every element in the lesson plan to one of the objectives. This technique will identify both extraneous materials in the program and necessary materials that are not covered.

- Set up a review committee to determine if the training that the vendor will provide will alleviate the hazards presented by the work. This committee should include some members of the safety council and some people who actually do the welding.

If more than one course is planned, use the first course as a pilot. Give the trainees opportunity to provide feedback to the vendor as to how the course can be improved to better fit their specific needs.

WRITING A LESSON PLAN

One essential instructional material is a written lesson plan (see Figure 6.1). A lesson plan should include the following elements:

- The course objectives

- At least an outline of all the information the instructor is to convey to the trainees

- A list of trainee activities and a description of how they are sequenced with the learning activities

STRUCTURING MATERIALS AND ACTIVITIES INTO THE TRAINING PROGRAM

Structure is the sequence in which the content and the various learning activities used to convey or reinforce the content are presented.

Imagine that you are an architect. You work for a company that

ORGANIZATION NAME

DEPARTMENT NAME

Module:	Page ____ of ____
Unit:	Author:
Approval:	Revision #:
Date:	Revision by:
Prerequisites:	References:
Estimated Teaching Time:	Target Population:
Instructional Media:	Instructional Methods:

LEARNING OBJECTIVES

1.

2.

3.

4.

5.

TITLE PAGE

FIGURE 6.1   A format for lesson plans.

builds modular homes. The company prebuilds kitchens, bedrooms, porches, living rooms, and so on, and you determine how they are assembled into a complete home. You have some influence over how the modules are built, but that influence is limited. Other factors exert greater influence over the construction of the modules, such as the materials available to the factory, the skills of the workers, and the budget

INSTRUCTOR ACTIVITIES	TRAINEE ACTIVITIES

INSIDE PAGES

FIGURE 6.1   (*Continued*)

allotted for materials and labor. Consider what factors would determine how you would assemble the houses:

- A major factor would be the desires of the company's customers, the people who bought the houses. If you had the opportunity to work with them directly, you would undoubtedly ask them many questions about their current needs, their plans for the future, and aspects of their life-style that might affect their living space.

An unmarried professional who worked out of his or her house and planned to remain single, for example, would have a much different house built than would a married couple with two children and plans for more, even if the two houses were going to be the same size.

- If you do not have this opportunity to custom design the houses for the occupants, you would need to do some serious market research to determine what the wants and needs of potential buyers were. Then you would design the homes to anticipate those needs.

- No matter what the wants or needs of the customers were, the house you designed would have to meet the budgetary constraints of the customers. No one would appreciate your efforts if you designed a beautiful house that was outside of their ability to pay.

- The house would have to meet federal, state, and local building codes.

- Of course, the house would have to be built out of the aforementioned modules.

This is a good analogy for the position of the safety program developer who has systematically determined the required content of the safety training and developed or selected instructional materials that contain this content.

The instructional materials are the components one has to work with, just as the architect works with the building materials. You had some control over those when they were developed or selected, but there were other overriding concerns, namely, the learning needs that were identified by the job hazard analysis, your skills and those of your codevelopers (if any), and the time and money allotted for the project.

A major factor that would shape the structure of the program would be the learning characteristics of the trainees. The safety program developers are at a great advantage if they have an intimate working relationship with the trainees. They can speak to them directly about what motivates them to learn, what learning modes and media work effectively for them, and what they have liked and disliked about various programs.

If the program developers do not have that opportunity (let's say that they work in the corporate office of a company that has far-flung manufacturing plants), success at structuring the training will require good assessment skills (just as the architect would need good market research skills). The same instructional content may be structured quite differently depending on the group that will be getting the training. The time allotted for the training will have a great deal to do with how it is structured, just as the money allotted for the house would determine how it is built. If the training had to take place during 40-minute segments in the plant, it would be structured quite differently than if it took place over one day in a classroom.

Just as the architect would need to comply with a host of building codes, the program developer must structure the program so that it complies with federal, state, and local regulations. In addition to those regulations, the program developers will want to comply with company policy and probably with "consensus standards," the recommendations of experts in the field.

For the most part these regulations affect the content, not the structure, of the program. But content directly affects structure in two ways. First, training, as defined by OSHA, involves an opportunity for interaction between the trainees and a live instructor; there has to be a question-and-answer period. Second, training for many safety and health programs includes a "hands-on" portion. Both question-and-answer sessions and hands-on training must be incorporated into the structure of the program. Adequate time (based on previous experience with the target population) and instructional materials must be allotted for the pilot program.

Finally, just as the architect must assemble the house out of the modules already constructed, the program developer must deal with the instructional materials (lecture outlines, tests, videos, demonstrations, skill measures, and so on) that have already been selected or developed because they meet the learning needs of the trainees.

In structuring the course, the program developer may decide that some changes in these materials will allow them to fit together more

GUIDELINES FOR SEQUENCING OF INSTRUCTION

1. *Work from simple to complex.* Some training concepts are easier to understand than others. As a general rule, put the easy stuff first. For example, during hazard communication training, start off by explaining what the rights of workers are. This is easier than explaining the structure of the Material Safety Data Sheet or the specific information on overexposures. If some of the material requires greater concentration, such as math skills, work up to it.

2. *Put preliminary information first.* Just as an architect does not build the roof before he builds the walls, the course designer does not present advanced skills or knowledge until the trainees are proficient in basic skills. In CPR training, for example, trainees are taught how to recognize a breathing emergency before they are taught mouth-to-mouth resuscitation, and they are taught mouth-to-mouth resuscitation before they are taught CPR.

3. *Work from the familiar to the unfamiliar.* The instructor who know what the trainees are already familiar with can use that knowledge to guide the trainees confidently into less familiar territory. If, for example, the trainees are seasoned asbestos abatement workers, start out with the hazards of asbestos itself, which they have undoubtedly heard about many times, then work into discussions of the other, less familiar hazards associated with asbestos removal, such as the toxic effects of the adhesives and encapsulants used in abatement.

4. *Start and end with motivational material.* Often, instructors will end a series of safety and health-related training programs with a motivational presentation of the general importance of safety. That may help trainees as they leave the classroom and enter the workplace, but it will do nothing to help them concentrate in class. Begin the class with some type of motivational presentation—something that helps them to relate personally to the material to come.

STRUCTURING OF INFORMATION WITHIN ONE PROGRAM

The guidelines presented above also apply when determining how to structure the information within one program. But there are other considerations, such as when to insert tests and how to sequence the hands-on and classroom portions.

Tests serve several purposes in education. The obvious one is to determine whether the student can be considered as having acquired the knowledge and skills described in the learning objectives. Other purposes are to:

- Provide feedback, during the training, to the trainees and/or the instructor as to the degree of the trainees' comprehension. This informs the trainees of what they have to study, and the instructor of where he or she should place this emphasis.

- Rank trainees when test performance is to be used as a factor in selection (for example, when selecting trainees for a new job or for a promotion).

The purposes of testing will be discussed at length in Chapter 8. The issue here is how to fit them into the structure of the course. The critical rule regarding when to insert a test is test to ensure comprehension of prerequisite skills. In other words, test whenever a point is reached in the training where comprehension of what has been taught previously is essential to understanding what will be taught. That is the central rule; do not lose the trainees. Another factor when structuring tests is to keep the class interesting by using tests to break sections of instruction and to build trainee self-confidence by providing opportunities for early successes.

1. List, and write brief definitions of, the three steps involved in developing learning activities.

2. List three characteristics of the target population that may affect how they learn.

3. List three ways of determining the learning characteristics of the target population.

4. Write an alternative to this chapter's definition of learning, or restate the definition in your own terms.

5. List three benefits of trainee evaluation.

6. List three different methods of structuring training sessions.

The operating manager has asked the training supervisor to develop or procure a training program on asbestos abatement.

7. What in-house equipment and expertise will be required if the training supervisor wishes to develop the training?

8. If the training supervisor procures a predeveloped training program, what steps should she take to ensure that the program meets the training needs of the employees?

9. State how the program should be structured, and justify your decision.

10. Should the training supervisor simply agree with the operating manager's assessment that asbestos removal training is needed? What are some questions the training supervisor should ask to determine if the operating manager has come to the correct conclusion?

 # REFERENCES

1. R. Mager and K. Beach, *Developing Vocational Instruction* (Belmont, CA: Pitman Management and Training, 1967).

2. Robert Gottschall, "Safety Management and Total Employee Health Costs, *Professional Safety* 35, no. 7 (July 1990):24–27. Published by American Society of Safety Engineers (ASSE), Desplaines, IL.

3. Mager and Beach, *Developing Vocational Instruction,* pp. 25–27.

CONDUCTING
THE
TRAINING

KEY CONCEPTS OF CHAPTER SEVEN

*T*he presentation must be geared to the values and learning styles of the trainees.

*I*t is important to keep the trainees mentally active. The safety instructor should work to keep the trainees periodically applying what they have learned to their specific responsibilities.

*T*wo common errors in safety training must be avoided: *unreasonable fears* of occupational hazards and *lack of fear* of occupational hazards.

The emphasis of this book is on developing, not presenting, safety training programs. But part of the development phase is evaluation, and some aspects of evaluation cannot take place until a course is presented.

Many of the guidelines for presenting training programs on safety apply equally well to any type of training, but there are special problems and opportunities that are specific to safety and health. Any consideration of what makes for effective safety instruction must begin with an understanding of what constitutes effective learning.

The classic behaviorist definition of learning is "any activity that changes behavior." That definition may be helpful for educational psychologists but is of no value for developers and instructors of safety and health training programs. If trainees walk out of a program bored or unconvinced that the skills or concepts presented apply to their work, there may well be an observable behavior change; the employee may take even more unacceptable risks than he or she did prior to the training! All training programs convey something to the trainees. If the presentation is haphazard or the instructor obviously uncaring, the unintended message of the training may be either "Management does not care about safety" or "There are no real risks associated with this work, so the training department is filling a requirement for periodic safety training." Therefore, safety instructors need a working definition of learning as it applies to the occupational environment. From the perspective of occupational safety, the definition of learning is:

Any activity that changes behavior so that the likelihood of learners becoming injured on the job is reduced.

OSHA defines training as "the planned and organized activity of a consultant to impart skills, techniques, and methodologies to employers and their employees to assist them in established and maintaining employment and a place of employment which is safe and healthful" (29 CFS 1908.2).

If workers leave the training session less likely to be injured than when they entered the training session, then the training was successful. They learned something! They meet OSHA's definition of training and learning. If their behavior on the job is not more safe after completion of training, the training program was unsuccessful. It is the change of behavior that determines the success of the training session, not the quality of the audiovisuals, nor the employees' rating of the course. In fact, some studies indicate a *negative* correlation between trainee success, as measured by test scores, and employee approval, as measured by trainee evaluation forms.[1]

Training is devoted to guiding the trainee into a specific learning experience. In the case of safety training, these learning experiences should be planned so that the trainee leaves the class meeting the learning objectives that were established during the job hazard analysis.

The following sections present a number of guidelines the safety instructor can follow that facilitate the transfer of knowledge from the instructor to the trainee.

GUIDELINES FOR CONDUCTING TRAINING

☐ START WITH A PILOT PROGRAM

Piloting a systematically developed training program is sometimes a pleasure. If course content has been well matched to the learning needs and learning styles of the trainees, the pilot program will almost certainly hold their interest. Still, unanticipated problems with content and presentation can occur after the most careful development process. Job responsibilities and employee assignments can change quickly, and an instructor may discover that the group of trainees assembled for the training program varies from the target population for whom the training was intended.

Because of these and other problems, the pilot program, although sometimes a pleasure, is always a necessity; it is the ultimate "reality check." The best-laid plans and the most carefully developed training may go astray, and the problems that caused it to do so must be conveyed to those who developed the training. Of course, if the developers attend the pilot, or better yet participate in the instruction, they will have the benefit of firsthand experience.

One developer who wrote a hazard communication training program for his company also had the opportunity to teach the pilot program. Although the course emphasized procuring and interpreting Material Safety Data Sheets, most of the trainees' questions were related to interpreting product labels. These labels were the trainees' primary source of information about the products with which they worked.

While teaching the pilot program, the developer noted that trainees paid closer attention when visual learning aids, such as transparencies or sample products, were used to support the lecture content. The program was therefore rewritten to place more emphasis on interpreting product labels, and more visual aids were incorporated into the presentation. Because of the importance of Material Safety Data Sheets in chemical hazard awareness, the revised training program also emphasized *why* trainees should review the sheets instead of only *how* to obtain and read them. This is a good example of the kind of "fine-tuning" of training that can only be accomplished through a pilot program.

☐ PERSONALIZE THE TRAINING

Relate the information presented during the training to the lives of the trainees. Soliciting anecdotes from the trainees is an excellent way to do this. It gives trainees an opportunity to participate, it briefly relieves the instructor of the pressure to perform, and the anecdotes have the added interest and credibility of being presented firsthand. The trainees can be asked to share their experiences with specific chemicals, processes, or pieces of equipment. Training can be personalized by relating it to the trainees' homes or occupational experience or to their values. Many of the safety guidelines taught on the job also apply outside the job. For example, teenagers are sensitive to appearance. Therefore, a presentation on the use of seat belts can capitalize on the value of appearance. Perhaps the trainer can hold up a seat belt and a picture of Freddy Krueger and say, "This is all that keeps you from winning a Freddy Krueger look-alike contest." Seat belt training for married adults might focus on their responsibility to protect their spouses and children. An appeal to older adults might emphasize the role of the seat belt in protecting their own mobility and the lives of their grandchildren.

☐ ALLOW FOR EARLY SUCCESSES IN TRAINING

The early evaluations and practice sessions should be easy enough to permit almost all trainees to succeed. This is a considerable morale builder and makes the trainee open to learning.

☐ HELP THE TRAINEE CONCENTRATE

This is extremely important. Much training time is wasted because the trainees lose concentration. Most people are simply not mentally capable of concentration for hours at a time. Anything the instructors can do to help trainees maintain concentration will win the instructors much goodwill. The room should be kept free of distractions. The classroom should be clean and attractive and free of superfluous teaching materials. Instructors should be dressed neatly, in attractive, noncontroversial clothing. Teaching safety and health is not the time to be making a fashion statement. If possible (it's probably not) make the classroom a "no-pager" zone. Some pagers can be set to vibrate instead of beep. Ask trainees to use that feature if their pagers have it.

If the instructor has any control over the location of the training facilities, he or she should select a site area away the noise of production, and where trainees are unlikely to be interrupted. The classroom temperature should be comfortable (ideally 68 to 70 °F) and the room should have adequate ventilation. Many industrial workers may have been out of a classroom environment for 20 years or more and they may initially be uncomfortable and easily distracted in the learning environment. If possible, provide coffee and doughnuts in the morning and soft drinks in the afternoon. The investment, if one compares it with the total cost of training, is minuscule, yet the payback is substantial. The refreshments help keep the trainees in the classroom instead of wandering off to vending machines. Better yet, provide a free lunch: it's great for morale, keeps the trainees together and talking to each, and ensures they will not return late. Amazingly, they often continue to talk about the subject being taught.

Most trainees' attention span has been conditioned by television. Note some time, while you are watching television, how often the images change and how much action is incorporated into those images. This is the kind of presentation the trainees are used to. While it may not be possible, or even desirable, for the instructor to duplicate a television presentation, there is much the instructor can do to prevent boredom. Information should be presented in discrete "chunks" that are interesting and comprehensible.

☐ SCHEDULE AMPLE BREAKS

It is unrealistic to expect trainees to concentrate on difficult material for more than an hour, or on easy material for more than a hour and a half. Breaks do not have to be long; ten minutes should suffice—enough time to stretch, clear one's mind, and use the bathroom if necessary. Trainees often "debrief"—ask questions and share concerns they were embarrassed or afraid to ask during class—during breaks. Getting these topics off their mind helps them concentrate.

☐ ALWAYS START WITH A REVIEW OF THE LEARNING OBJECTIVES

One of the best ways to help trainees learn is to clearly convey what is expected of them. Fortunately, these expectations are already clearly articulated in the learning objectives. Start every presentation with a review of the learning objectives. For each objective presented, provide at least one benefit of the trainee meeting the objective. If you cannot come up with a least one benefit, the objective is questionable and the instructor should reconsider whether it belongs in the program. These benefits should relate to performance on the job and should be stated positively: "The CPR skills you learn today may save the life of your best friend, child, or spouse" not "If you don't pass this CPR class, you will not be eligible for a promotion." Information like the latter should be passed on to the students, but it should not be relied on for motivation.

☐ EMPHASIZE DECISION-MAKING SKILLS

Informing workers of the occupational hazards they may encounter is an important component of safety training, but in itself is inadequate. Workers in an industrial environment will be encountering situations that were not specifically covered in class. Responding to these situations in a safe manner requires that they understand underlying principles well enough to apply them; that they have the necessary discernment to know when to act on their own and when to seek expert advice; and that they have the information necessary to make reasoned decisions and the confidence to act on them. If workers are to make, and act on, reasoned decisions, they must first be able to assess potentially hazardous situations and evaluate the degree of risk. Assessment, evaluation, and decision-making all can be learned through guided practice. Through both casual questions and formal exercises, an effective instructor will provide trainees with opportunities to make decisions regarding acceptable risk.

☐ DON'T TERRORIZE THE TRAINEES!

This is a special problem that is unique to safety and health training. One effective method of getting the trainees' attention is to tell them a true story about an employee who was injured as a result of violating a safety rule. Sadly, stories like this are not difficult to obtain. This is an effective technique, but it should be used cautiously and sparingly. Many OSHA regulations, notably the hazard communication standard (29 CFS 1910.1200), require that management notify workers of the risks associated with their work. This standard in particular mandates that trainees be informed of the hazards of exposure to chemicals and other substances used on the job.

The most common way to present this information is to review each chemical's Material Safety Data Sheets (see Figure 7.1). Many of the sheets, even for substances considered relatively innocuous, are quite upsetting when describing the consequences of overexposure. Words and phrases like *cancer, fetotoxin, nervous system damage, blindness,* and *severe injury or death* abound. Most trainees understand the context of these terms: that they describe the effects of overexposure, but there will be exceptions.

When holding classes that communicate hazards to workers, the instructor must address two classes of workers: *Fearless Freds* and *Hysterical Harrys.* Fearless Freds are the trainees who do not take occupational hazard warnings seriously, and consequently are a threat to themselves, their co-workers, and the company. They are the ones who casually poke a hole in their respirator to permit entry of their cigarette, or wash their hands in the nearest available organic solvent.

Hysterical Harrys represent the other extreme: workers who overreact to perceived threats to their health or safety. Often their concerns are exacerbated by reports about occupational hazards in the news media. Unfounded anxiety about occupational hazards may hamper productivity, undermine morale, and even cause work stoppages. Hysterical

Genium Publishing Corp.	**Material Safety Data Sheets Collection**	
One Genium Plaza Schenectady, NY 12304-4690 (518)377-8854	Acetone	**MSDS No. 300**
	Issued: 11/77	Revision: F, 9/92

Section 1 - Chemical Product and Company Identification 39

Material Name..................... Acetone
Chemical Formula .... CH_3COCH_3
CAS No. 67-64-1
Other Designations: AI3-01238, Chevron acetone, dimethylformaldehyde, dimethylketal, dimethyl ketone, ß-ketopropane, methyl ketone, propanone, 2-propanone, pyroacetic acid, pyroacetic ether.
Derivation: Derived by the dehydrogenation or oxidation of isopropyl alcohol with a metallic catalyst, the oxidation of cumene, the vapor phase oxidation of butane; and as a by-product of synthetic glycerol production.
Use: Used as a solvent for paint, varnish, lacquer, fat, oil, wax, resin, rubber, plastic, and rubber cement; to clean and dry parts of precision equipment; in the manufacture of chemicals (methyl isobutyl ketone, methyl isobutyl carbinol, methyl methacrylate, bisphenol-A, acetic acid (ketene process), mesityl oxide, diacetone alcohol, chloroform, iodoform, bromoform), explosives, airplane dopes, rayon, photographic films, isoprene; acetylene gas storage cylinders; in purifying paraffin; in nail polish remover; in the extraction of various principles from animal and plant substances; in hardening and dehydrating tissues; in cellulose acetate (especially as spinning solvent); as a solvent for potassium iodide and permanganate; as a delusterant for cellulose acetate fibers; in the plasticity testing of vulcanized rubber products.
Manufacturer: Contact your supplier or distributor. Consult the latest *Chemical Week Buyers' Guide*[(73)] for a suppliers list.

Section 2 - Composition / Information on Ingredients

Acetone: 99.5%, 0.5% Water

1991 OSHA PELs *	**1990 NIOSH REL**	**1990 DFG (Germany) MAK**
8-hr TWA: 750 ppm (1,800 mg/m^3)	TWA: 250 ppm (590 mg/m^3)	1,000 ppm (2,400 mg/m^3)
15-min STEL: 1,000 ppm (2,400 mg/m^3)		Category IV: Substances eliciting very weak effects (MAK > 500 mL/m^3)
1992-93 ACGIH TLVs	**1990 IDLH Level**	Peak: 2,000 ppm, 60 min, momentary
TWA: 750 ppm (1,780 mg/m^3)	20,000 ppm	value,[†] 3 peaks/shift
STEL: 1,000 ppm (2,380 mg/m^3)		

* In the cellulose acetate fiber industry, enforcement of the OSHA TWA for "doffers" was stayed on 9/5/89 until 9/1/90; the OSHA STEL *does not* apply to that industry.
[†] Momentary value is a level which the concentration should never exceed.

Section 3 - Hazards Identification

> ☆☆☆☆☆ **Emergency Overview** ☆☆☆☆☆
> Colorless, highly volatile liquid; sweetish odor. Acetone vapor is a dangerous fire and explosion hazard. High vapor concentrations may produce narcosis (unconsciousness). Prolonged or repeated skin contact causes dryness, irritation, and mild dermatitis.

Wilson Risk Scale	
R	1
I	1
S	1*
K	3

* Slight skin absorption

HMIS	
H	1
F	3
R	0
PPE[†]	

[†]Sec. 8

Potential Health Effects

Carcinogenicity: IARC, NTP, and OSHA do not list acetone as a carcinogen.
Summary of Risks: Acetone has been placed among solvents of comparatively low acute and chronic toxicities. In industry, the most common effects reported are headache from prolonged vapor inhalation and skin irritation resulting from its defatting action. Exposure to less than 1,000 ppm acetone vapor produces only slight eye, nose, and throat irritation. Acetone does not have sufficient warning properties to prevent repeated exposures. It is narcotic at high concentrations (above 2,000 ppm). Concentrations above 12,000 ppm cause loss of consciousness.
Medical Conditions Aggravated by Long-Term Exposure: None reported.
Target Organs: Respiratory and central nervous systems, skin.
Primary Entry Routes: Inhalation, skin and eye contact, ingestion. Liquid acetone is slowly absorbed through the skin.
Acute Effects:
Eye: Direct eye contact by liquid acetone may produce painful burning and stinging; watering of eyes; conjunctival inflammation; and corneal injury.
Skin: Skin contact produces a cold feeling, dryness, and mild irritation.
Inhalation: Human systemic effects by inhalation include eye, nose, and throat irritation; nausea and vomiting; changes in EEG (electroencephalogram) and carbohydrate metabolism; muscle weakness; drunken behavior; mental confusion and visual disturbance. In extreme cases, breathing high concentrations may produce coma.
Ingestion: Human systemic effects by ingestion include gastrointestinal irritation, kidney damage (often indicated by albumin and red and white blood cells in urine), liver damage (indicated by high levels of urobilin and early appearance of bilirubin),

FIGURE 7.1 Typical Material Safety Data Sheets (*Courtesy of Genium Publishing Corporation.*)

Harrys, for example, may refuse to proceed with a job because they are in the vicinity of wrapped insulation that may contain asbestos, or across from a computer monitor that may be emitting excessive radiation. Are they exercising their right to a safe workplace, or are they unnecessarily stopping a critical job?

Acute Effects (cont.):
coma, metabolic changes, and systemic effects described for inhalation.
Chronic effects: Cases of chronic poisoning resulting from prolonged exposure to low concentrations of acetone are rare. Workers exposed to 1,000 ppm, 3 hr per day for 7-15 yr, complained of dizziness, asthenia (lack or loss of strength), and chronic inflammation of the airways, stomach, and duodenum. Prolonged or repeated skin contact with liquid acetone may defat the skin and cause eczematoid dermatitis.

Section 4 - First Aid Measures

Eyes: *Do not* allow victim to rub or keep eyes tightly shut. Gently lift eyelids and flush immediately and continuously with flooding amounts of water until transported to an emergency medical facility. Consult a physician immediately.
Skin: *Quickly* remove contaminated clothing. Rinse with flooding amounts of water for at least 15 min. Wash exposed area with soap and water. For reddened or blistered skin, consult a physician. Carefully dispose of contaminated clothing because it may pose a fire hazard.
Inhalation: Remove exposed person to fresh air, monitor for respiratory distress and administer 100% humidified supplemental oxygen as needed.
Ingestion: Never give anything by mouth to an unconscious or convulsing person. Contact a poison control center. Unless the poison control center advises otherwise, have that *conscious and alert* person drink 1 to 2 glasses of water, then induce vomiting.
After first aid, get appropriate in-plant, paramedic, or community medical support.
Note to Physicians: In symptomatic patients, monitor serum and urine acetone levels, fluid intake, blood glucose, and arterial pH. Because of the prolonged elimination half-life of acetone, the symptomatic patient may need medical supervision for many hours (up to 30 hr). Patients may develop hyperglycemia and ketosis mimicking acute diabetic coma. The hyperglycemia may persist for several days following acute exposure.

Section 5 - Fire Fighting Measures

Flash Point .... 0°F (-18°C), CC
Autoignition Temperature .... 869°F (465°C)
LEL .... 2.6% v/v
UEL .... 12.8% v/v

NFPA

$$\begin{array}{c} 3 \\ 1 \quad \diamond \quad 0 \\ - \end{array}$$

Extinguishing Media: *Do not* extinguish fire unless flow can be stopped. For small fires, use dry chemical, carbon dioxide (CO_2), water spray, or alcohol-resistant foam. For large fires, use water spray, fog, or alcohol-resistant foam. Use water in flooding quantities as fog because solid streams may be ineffective.
Unusual Fire or Explosion Hazards: Acetone is a dangerous fire and explosion hazard; it is a Class IB flammable liquid. Vapors may travel to a source of ignition and flash back. Fire-exposed containers may explode. A vapor explosion hazard may exist indoors, outdoors, or, in sewers.
Fire-Fighting Instructions: If feasible, remove all fire-exposed containers. Otherwise, apply cooling water to sides of containers until well after fire is extinguished. If the fire becomes uncontrollable or container is exposed to direct flame, consider evacuation of a one-third mile radius. In case of rising sound from venting safety device or any discoloration of tank during fire, withdraw immediately. Do not release runoff from fire control methods to sewers or waterways.
Fire-Fighting Equipment: Because fire may produce toxic thermal decomposition products, wear a self-contained breathing apparatus (SCBA) with a full facepiece operated in pressure-demand or positive-pressure mode. Structural firefighters' protective clothing provides limited protection. For massive cargo fires, use unmanned hose holder or monitor nozzles.

Section 6 - Accidental Release Measures

Spill / Leak Procedures: Notify safety personnel, evacuate all unnecessary personnel, remove all heat and ignition sources and provide adequate ventilation. Cleanup personnel should protect against inhalation and skin or eye contact. If feasible and without risk, stop leak. Use water spray to reduce vapor but it may not prevent ignition in closed spaces.
Small Spills: For small spills, take up with sand or other noncombustible absorbent material and using nonsparking tools, place into containers for later disposal.
Large Spills: For large spills, dike far ahead of liquid spill for later disposal. Do not release into sewers or waterways. Follow applicable OSHA regulations (29 CFR 1910.120).

Section 7 - Handling and Storage

Storage Requirements: Store in closed containers in a cool, dry, well-ventilated area away from heat, sparks, flames, and other incompatibles. Keep large stocks away from inhabited buildings.
Handling Precautions: Use nonsparking tools to open containers. Keep dry chemical or CO_2 extinguishers on hand in case of fire.

FIGURE 7.1   *(Continued)*

CHEMICAL DOSE AND RELATIVE RISK

A key to avoiding both underreaction and overreaction to potential hazards is thoroughly training workers in the concepts of dose and relative risk. *Dose* is the amount of a substance to which a worker is exposed

Section 8 - Exposure Controls / Personal Protection

Engineering Controls: To prevent static sparks, electrically ground and bond all containers and equipment during fluid transfer. For bulk storage rooms, install electrical equipment, Class I, Group D.

Ventilation: Provide general and local exhaust ventilation systems to maintain airborne concentrations below OSHA PELs (Sec. 2). Local exhaust ventilation is preferred because it prevents contaminant dispersion into the work area by controlling it at its source.[103]

Administrative Controls: Consider preplacement and periodic medical examinations with emphasis on the skin and respiratory tract. Also consider liver and kidney function tests and urinalysis.

Protective Clothing/Equipment: Wear chemically protective gloves, boots, aprons, and gauntlets to prevent prolonged or repeated skin contact. Polyethylene/ethylene vinyl alcohol, Teflon, or butyl rubber with breakthrough times > 8 hr is recommended for PPE. Wear protective eyeglasses or chemical safety goggles, per OSHA eye- and face-protection regulations (29 CFR 1910.133). Because contact lens use in industry is controversial, establish your own policy.

Respirator: Seek professional advice prior to respirator selection and use. Follow OSHA respirator regulations (29 CFR 1910.134) and, if necessary, wear a MSHA/NIOSH-approved respirator. Select respirator based on its suitability to provide adequate worker protection for given working conditions, level of airborne contamination, and presence of sufficient oxygen. For concentrations < 1,000 ppm, wear any chemical cartridge respirator with organic vapor cartridge(s) and wear eye protection to avoid irritation or damage. For concentrations < 6,250 ppm, wear any supplied-air respirator operated in a continuous-flow mode. For concentrations < 12,500 ppm, wear any air-purifying, full-facepiece respirator (gas mask) with a chin-style, front- or back-mounted organic vapor canister. For concentrations < 20,000 ppm, wear any supplied-air respirator that has a full facepiece and is operated in a pressure-demand or other positive-pressure mode. For emergency or nonroutine operations (cleaning spills, reactor vessels, or storage tanks), wear an SCBA. *Warning! Air-purifying respirators do not protect workers in oxygen-deficient atmospheres.* If respirators are used, OSHA requires a written respiratory protection program that includes at least: medical certification, training, fit-testing, periodic environmental monitoring, maintenance, inspection, cleaning, and convenient, sanitary storage areas.

Safety Stations: Make available in the work area emergency eyewash stations, safety/quick-drench showers, and washing facilities.

Contaminated Equipment: Separate contaminated work clothes form street clothes. Launder before reuse. Remove this material from your shoes and clean personal protective equipment.

Comments: Never eat, drink, or smoke in work areas. Practice good personal hygiene after using this material, especially before eating, drinking, smoking, using the toilet, or applying cosmetics.

Section 9 - Physical and Chemical Properties

Physical State.................... Liquid
Color................................Colorless
Odor .... Sweet
Odor Threshold................47.5 mg/m^3 to 1,613.9 mg/m^3 *
Boiling Point .... 133.2°F (56.2°C) at 760 mm Hg
Freezing Point ....-139.6°F (-95.35°C)
Refractive Index...............1.3588 @ 20°C
Water Solubility ....Soluble
Molecular Weight 58.08

Other Solubilities............. Alcohol, benzene, dimethyl formamide, chloroform, ether, and most oils
Specific Gravity .... 0.7889 @ 20°C /4°C
Vapor Pressure .... 180 mm Hg at 68°F (20°C) 400 mm Hg at 103.1°F (39.5°C)
Saturated Vapor Density . (Air = 1.2 kg/m^3, 0.075 lb/ft^3 1.48 kg/m^3, .093 lb/ft^3

* Odor thresholds recorded as a range from the lowest to the highest concentration.

Section 10 - Stability and Reactivity

Stability: Acetone is stable at room temperature in closed containers under normal storage and handling conditions.

Polymerization: Hazardous polymerization cannot occur.

Chemical Incompatibilities: Acetone may form explosive mixtures with hydrogen peroxide, acetic acid, nitric acid, nitric acid + sulfuric acid, chromic anhydride, chromyl chloride, nitrosyl chloride, hexachloromelamine, nitrosyl perchlorate, nitryl perchlorate, permonosulfuric acid, thiodiglycol + hydrogen peroxide. Acetone reacts vigorously with oxidizing materials and ignites on contact with activated carbon, chromium trioxide, dioxygen difluoride + carbon dioxide, and potassium-*tert*-butoxide. Other incompatibles include air, bromoform, bromine, chloroform + alkalis, trichloromelamine, and sulfur dichloride.

Conditions to Avoid: Keep acetone away from plastic eyeglass frames, jewelry, pens, pencils, and rayon garments.

Hazardous Products of Decomposition: Thermal oxidative decomposition of acetone can produce CO_2 and carbon monoxide (CO).

FIGURE 7.1   *(Continued)*

over a given amount of time. When discussing hazardous materials, we are specifically interested in what dose of a chemical may have adverse health effects. There are two categories of doses about which safety instructors should educate trainees: doses that can cause acute (over a short

Section 11- Toxicological Information

Toxicity Data:*

Eye Effects:
Human, eye: 500 ppm

Acute Oral Effects:
Rat, oral, LD_{50}: 5800 mg/kg altered sleep time and produced tremors.

Acute Inhalation Effects:
Human, inhalation, TC_{Lo}: 500 ppm produced olfaction effects, conjunctival irritation, and other changes involving the lungs, thorax, or respiration.
Mammal, inhalation, TC_{Lo}: 31,500 $\mu g/m^3/24$ hr administered to pregnant female from the 1st to 13th day of gestation produced effects on fertility (post-implantation mortality).

* See NIOSH, *RTECS* (AL3150000), for additional irritation, mutation, reproductive, and toxicity data.

Section 12 - Ecological Information

Ecotoxicity: LC_{50} *Salmo gairdneri* (rainbow trout): 5,540 mg/L/96 hr at 54°F (12°C).
LC_{50} (oral) Ring-necked pheasant: > 40,000 ppm.
Environmental Degradation: Acetone biodegrades when released into the environment. The biological oxygen demand for 5 days (BOD5) is 46-55%.
Soil Absorption / Mobility: Acetone volatilizes, leaches, and biodegrades if released on soil.

Section 13 - Disposal Considerations

Disposal: Acetone is a good candidate for fluidized bed, rotary kiln incineration, or catalytic oxidation. Contact your supplier or a licensed contractor for detailed recommendations. Follow applicable Federal, state, and local regulations.

Section 14 - Transport Information

Transportation Data (49 CFR 172.101):

DOT Shipping Name...... Acetone
DOT Hazard Class........ 3
ID No. UN1090
DOT Packing Group II
DOT Label .... Flammable
                              Liquid
Special Provisions (172.102) T8

Packaging Authorizations:
a) Exceptions.....................173.150
b) Non-bulk Packaging..... 173.202
c) Bulk Packaging 173.242

Quantity Limitations:
a) Passenger, Aircraft, or Railcar ...5L
b) Cargo Aircraft Only...... 60L

Vessel Stowage Requirements:
a) Vessel Stowage .... B
b) Other............................. —

Section 15 - Regulatory Information

EPA Designations:
Listed as a RCRA Hazardous Waste (40 CFR 261.33): Hazardous Waste No. U002 (Ignitability), (40 CFR 261.31): F003 (spent solvent)
Listed as a CERCLA Hazardous Substance* (40 CFR 302.4): Final Reportable Quantity (RQ), 5,000 lb (2,270 kg) [* per Clean Water Act, Sec. 311(b)(4)]
SARA Extremely Hazardous Substance (40 CFR 355): Not listed
Listed as a SARA Toxic Chemical (40 CFR 372.65)
OSHA Designations:
Listed as an Air Contaminant (29 CFR 1910.1000, Table Z-1-A)

Section 16 - Other Information

MSDS Collection References: 26, 73, 100, 101, 103, 124, 126, 127, 132, 133, 136, 139, 140, 148, 149, 153, 159, 163, 164, 167, 168, 171, 174, 176, 180.

Prepared by .... M. J. Wurth, BS
Industrial Hygiene Review .... P. A. Roy, MPH, CIH
Medical Review .... A. C. Darlington, MPH, MD

Disclaimer: Judgments as to the suitability of information herein for the purchaser's purposes are necessarily the purchaser's responsibility. Although reasonable care has been taken in the preparation of such information, Genium Publishing Corporation extends no warranties, makes no representations, and assumes no responsibility as to the accuracy or suitability of such information for application to the purchaser's intended purpose or for consequences of its use.

FIGURE 7.1   (*Continued*)

duration) reactions, and doses that cause chronic (over a long duration) reactions.

As analytical techniques improve, scientists are able to detect increasingly small amounts of chemicals. These chemicals show up in lists of the ingredients included in Material Safety Data Sheets. Most of the chemicals are harmful to humans at some level. Many may be known toxins or carcinogens. It is critical that those people using the chemicals know at what dose the chemicals are harmful.

Many cleaning chemicals, for example, contain chlorine, the active ingredient in bleach. Chlorine is hazardous if inhaled or absorbed through the skin. It also can be detrimental environmentally. The Material Safety Data Sheet for chlorine warns that overexposure may result in blindness, respiratory system damage, and cancer. Workers should know of these risks. It is important, however, that they also understand that OSHA has assigned permissible exposure limits (PELs), ceiling limits, and immediately dangerous to life and health (IDLH) limits for chlorine and most common industrial chemicals. All three of these terms relate to the doses of chemicals at which they present a health risk. Trainees who understand these terms will probably leave a hazard communications training session with a prudent and realistic attitude regarding workplace chemical exposures.

The *permissible exposure limit* is the amount of a chemical, averaged over eight hours, above which a worker shall not be exposed. The *ceiling limit* is, according to OSHA, the level of a chemical that "shall not be exceeded for any part of the work day" (20 CFS 1910.1000). Companies are required by law to keep exposures below these limits. OSHA has other criteria for evaluating chemical exposures, but these two will be most helpful to trainees.

An example will help differentiate between the two exposure limits. Workers may exceed the permissible exposure limit of a chemical over a few hours if they will not be exposed over the rest of the day, and if their average exposure during the day, when the hours of exposure and the hours of nonexposure are averaged, is not above the permissible exposure limit. Someone with a background in industrial hygiene would be capable of calculating these levels. Workers should never, even for a short length of time, be exposed to a chemical above the ceiling limit, even if, when averaged with the rest of the day, the exposure is low or nonexistent. That is because exposure over the ceiling limit may cause some type of harm to employees, even if there is no immediate reaction. Companies are required by law to keep employee exposures below permissible exposure and ceiling limits. While it is possible that some employees may have a special sensitivity or an allergy that causes them to have adverse reactions even if these limits are not exceeded, the limits have been derived very conservatively and, if respected, will protect nearly all workers from exposure-related injuries or illnesses.

The immediately dangerous to life and health (IDLH) level places the employee at great risk. The employee who is exposed, unprotected, to IDLH levels of a chemical must be removed from that environment.

Why are industrial hygiene concepts necessary to workers as part of their safety and health training? The workers need to understand, both for their personal protection and for their morale, that they are not being exposed to hazardous doses of chemicals, and that any substance, even water, can be hazardous at too high of a dose. On the other hand, maintaining morale, worker health, and productivity requires that jobs be designed so that workers are not exposed to chemicals at unsafe levels, and training is designed so that workers *understand* that they are not being exposed at unsafe levels.

Ammonia, sodium hydroxide, sodium chloride, and peroxides are all potentially unsafe chemicals. Whether that potential risk becomes a reality depends on the dose to which the users are exposed. Whether that dose is controlled to within safe limits depends on the design of the equipment, the procedures the worker follows, and the protective equipment he or she is wearing. Training workers on the concept of dosage and on the specific permissible exposure limits of the chemicals with which they work, and then monitoring their exposure and notifying them of the results, will help to eliminate the numbers of both Fearless Freds and Hysterical Harrys in the workplace. Trainees will instead have a reasonable grasp of the real health and safety risks in the workplace and an understanding of how to minimize those risks. In addition, the company would be meeting both the letter and the spirit of the OSHA hazard communications standard.

Put the above information in context, for example, training on back safety. Start off with some statistics on the number of back injuries annually, or review the physiology of the back and how it is affected by injuries. This information may not be necessary to impart the specific knowledge and skills for which the course was intended, but it makes the essential information more interesting, and encouraging the trainees to pay attention is the name of the game.

PRESENTATION GUIDELINES

An experienced instructor follows these guidelines:[2]

- Deliver only the quantity of material that your listeners need to know.

- Get rid of professional terminology.

- Keep in mind that audiences tend to remember narrative chunks more than they remember sophisticated, abstract information.

- Place the information you are presenting in a larger, interesting context.

- Stay physically close to your listeners whenever possible.

- Appear to have fun, even be theatrical, if necessary. Learning is difficult enough.

The effectiveness of the presentation depends on the trainees as well as the instructor. The trainees will be much more open to learning if the instructor succeeds in eliciting a sense of disequilibrium among them. "Disequilibrium" is the state of being out of balance. In terms of learning theory, it means the condition of not being able to do something new that one desires to do, or not being able to maintain some behavior that one was able to do in the past.

Many educational psychologists believe that disequilibrium is essential to learning, and that no learning takes place unless trainees are in this state. That is why it is essential for the instructor to provide motivation to learn. Once the trainees view the learning objectives of the course as being desirable, and once they understand that they do not already have these skills, they are in a state of disequilibrium. One of the many benefits of a pretest is that it helps the trainees to realize that they do not (in most cases) already know the material that is to be presented.

The importance of writing learning objectives and communicating them clearly to the trainees is well established in training texts. It is less well established, but equally important, that the instructor communicate a benefit to the trainees for mastering each of these objectives. As with establishing a performance, condition, and standard, establishing a benefit will sometimes be so obvious it need not be stated, such as when teaching the Heimlich maneuver, a technique for rescuing a choking victim. At other times, establishing a benefit may be quite difficult, such as when teaching some company procedure with which many of the trainees disagree.

As with the other components of a well-designed safety training program, the instructor should refer back to the original job hazard analysis to determine the benefits of mastering the skills and knowledge in the program.

Once trainees perceive the benefit of a particular objective, and the deficiency in performance is established (the trainee does not already possess the skills and knowledge required by that objective), disequilibrium has been achieved. This aspect of initiating a presentation is, much to the detriment of the training that goes on afterward, often overlooked. Benefits relate to values, and if the developer was systematic, values should have been determined during the study of the target population. Of course, the development of the training and the presentation of the training may be separated by both time and distance.

The instructor making the presentation may not have the luxury of relying on a target population analysis made by some other person at an earlier date. The instructor probably has a thorough understanding of the values of the trainees if the instructor and trainees work in the same facility. Instructors who travel to various sites should do some homework, if possible, and familiarize themselves with the target population before arriving. If that does not happen, the instructor should at least try to mingle with the trainees during breaks and lunch (one more reason to provide drinks and cater lunch if possible).

Training programs do not come with automatic credibility. Anything that adds to the program's credibility will enhance the presentation. One way to do this is to solicit the support of upper management. Executives introducing training programs are the closest thing to "instant credibility." What the executive says is not as important as the message that he or she sends by taking the time to open the training and the trouble to prepare a brief presentation.

While the safety instruction need not be easy, or even necessarily entertaining (although being entertaining helps), it must be a positive experience for the trainees if it is going to result in meaningful behavior changes. "Positive" here means that the training experience must result in personal satisfaction, not in personal pain or discomfort. If the trainees are bored, which is discomforting, or embarrassed, which is painful, they will avoid the specific behaviors that the trainers are trying to encourage.

Many adults have unpleasant memories of being ridiculed by teachers during their elementary or secondary education. These memories linger long into adulthood and are one reason that many adults feel anxiety about being in a classroom environment. An otherwise effective presentation can be severely undermined if, during a misguided attempt at humor, the instructor repeats mistakes made previously by cruel or thoughtless teachers.

One of the least effective ways of conveying information is to tell people they "should" do something, as if they are morally obligated to do so. Example: "You should always wear your hardhat." Or worse yet: "You should always be safe." At least in the first example a specific, observable behavior is described. Why doesn't this work? The trainee is not provided with a benefit for performing the behavior.

If the trainees are going to repeat the desirable behaviors that are presented in the classroom, they must first learn those behaviors. An effective presenter will ensure that new information is not discussed until the trainees already understand the information currently being presented. Although this can be partially accomplished during the structuring of the course, by building in frequent opportunities for evaluation, the final pace of the instruction is controlled by the presenter.

An effective presenter will frequently ask questions of the trainees to determine whether they are following the lecture. The presenter also will be alert for nonverbal cues, such as expressions of anxiety or confusion. He or she may overhear trainees talking to other trainees, trying to get clarification of what is being taught.

Any instructional aids that help the trainee to mentally organize or visualize what is being taught will increase the possibility that learning takes place. One helpful organizational aid is to start the presentation with a review of the objectives. The trainee then knows what to listen for and understands the instructor's expectations for performance.

Presentation outlines are a considerable aid to student concentration. Trying to summarize everything an instructor says will be difficult for most trainees and impossible for some. If an outline of the instructor's lecture is provided, however, the student only needs to take a few supplemental notes to elaborate on the outline. When students need to refer back to what was learned in the course they have, instead of just hand-written notes, a clearly written, typed outline from which to work. Another benefit of this format is that, should the trainees' concentration slip, they can use the notes to mentally "catch up" with the lecturer. In some classes where the material is progressive—that is, the instructor is continually introducing concepts that build on previous concepts—a momentary lapse of concentration can result in several hours of wasted training. The lecture notes can help avoid that, as will periodic quizzes and ample opportunity for questions and answers.

Presentation is absolutely as important as any other component of training. With the exception of self-instructional programs, there is no such thing as a "teacher-proof" course, in which the curriculum is so effective that the instructor cannot undermine its value through bad delivery. On the other hand, competent instructors can, even with poor teaching materials, guide the trainees through a meaningful learning experience. Therefore, consider instructor training as important as any other investment required for safety training. Many companies and universities offer "train the trainer" seminars. Find a company that has people who express interest in your operation and are willing to tailor their materials to your needs.

CHAPTER SEVEN **REVIEW AND APPLICATION**

1. Write some techniques that can be used to personalize the training.

2. Write some techniques that will allow for early successes.

3. Write some techniques that will help the trainee concentrate.

4. What are the groups within your organization that would have valuable recommendations regarding the content of this program? Were their recommendations solicited?

5. Early in the training, the instructor should:
   a. Evaluate the trainees
   b. Review the learning objectives
   c. Solicit trainee feedback on the effectiveness of instruction
   d. Schedule a break

6. List all the available resources for determining the tasks that this safety training should address. Exclude those already mentioned in question 5.

7. List two accurate sources of information regarding hazardous chemicals that are (or should be) readily available to workers, and may be used as instructional aids.

8. Define *Permissible Exposure Limit* (PEL).
   a. Amount of a chemical, averaged over eight hours, above which OSHA forbids exposure
   b. Degree of occupational risk as limited by OSHA's accident- prevention standard
   c. A contract between management and nonmanagement personnel regarding acceptable exposures in the work environment
   d. Tasks whose risk level is established, through a job hazard analysis, as being permissible

9. Define *IDLH*.
   a. Imminent damage limits for health
   b. Illness and life-damaging hazards
   c. Industrial definitions of living hazards
   d. Immediately dangerous to life and health

10. Explain, in a short paragraph, how understanding the concepts of risk and dose help prevent workers from either over- or underreacting to occupational hazards.

REFERENCES

1. Cyril O. Houle, *Continuing Learning in the Professions* (San Francisco: Jossey-Bass, 1981), 244–246.

2. Arnold Zenker, "Speaking of Speaking," *Training and Development* 46, no. 4 (April 1992):19.

EVALUATING PROGRAM EFFECTIVENESS

KEY CONCEPTS OF CHAPTER EIGHT

*T*rainee evaluation must be derived from the program learning objectives, not the course content.

*T*esting should be in the same domain of learning as was the training.

*T*est anxiety, a generalized fear of any evaluation of learning, can be reduced through fair and humane testing methods.

Every time an audience applauds, a bowling score is tabulated, a test is graded, or a shopper selects some cut flowers, leaving others behind, an evaluation is taking place. Evaluation plays a role in every on- and off-the-job decision we make, whether it is deciding if a trainee is able to perform a certain job responsibility safely or deciding whom to marry.

Most people think of educational evaluation in terms of testing the trainees' retention of the information or skills conveyed during a training program. This is a limited view of evaluation that will not result in the best possible safety training within the financial, resource, and time constraints in which the safety training developer must work. Safety training is most effective when the entire program development and implementation process, not just trainee performance, is subject to ongoing evaluation.

Evaluation of trainee performance is critical, but it is effective only to the extent that the training that preceded it was meaningful (that is, it addressed legitimate safety and health concerns). That training will be far more meaningful if all the steps in the training development and implementation process are evaluated.

In spite of all the benefits of evaluation, it is not carried out as regularly as it should, because most people, including trainees, intuitively resist having their performance evaluated. Most people, for example, feel threatened when asked to take a test. This feeling may be relatively mild and quickly mastered by those who are used to an academic environment, or may be overwhelming in those who have not been subject to testing for many years. While instructors cannot be certain of assuaging this fear, there are techniques they can use that will help most trainees, such as building up to final tests with small, easier quizzes, and avoiding assigning unnecessary consequences to test results.

Will failing the test mean losing one's job, not getting a promotion, or not being permitted to take on some new responsibility? If the training has been properly developed to meet legitimate performance needs, these are all possibilities. However, if keeping one's job or being promoted is actually based (as it invariably is) on a number of other factors that are not related to the test performance, then it would be poor management, as well as being lazy, unethical, and probably illegal, to make a test the sole criterion of performance.

Testing of trainees must be done in the context of complete course evaluation. Evaluation and fairness should go hand in hand. It would be unfair to test the trainees if the:

- *Course development process had not been evaluated,* because the skills being tested would likely not be related to the job.

- *Course materials had not been evaluated,* because poor performance on a test may very well actually be a result of the training both being tailored to the learning speed, style, and other characteristics of the trainee, not because the trainee cannot master the material.

- *Performance of the instructor is not evaluated,* since poor test performance would reflect the inability of the instructor to convey information, not the inability of the trainee to learn.

Evaluation is a package deal; fair and appropriate evaluation of the trainees requires that all elements of the program have been evaluated against several standards, such as:

- Does the training match the trainees' needs for performing the job safely?

- Is the training matched to the trainees' learning style?

- Are the performance requirements of the training reasonable?

Because these three elements are tied so closely to program improvement, they will be covered in Chapter 9, "Improving the Program." This chapter will focus on evaluating the success of the program in causing the worker to behave more safely on the job.

 ## MATCHING THE EVALUATION TO THE TRAINING

The best evaluation is the one that provides the instructor with useful information, not only on how the trainees performed on the test, but also on how they will perform on the job as a result of the training. To ensure that this happens, the test must be carefully derived from the learning objectives. Exactly what does this mean? For one thing, it means that the test developer should not derive test questions from the instructional material. The instructional material may include some "nice to know" information as well as the "need to know" information. "Nice to know" information is that which the instructor included to improve the continuity of the presentation, pique the trainees' interest, or reduce tension during a class. Common examples are anecdotal and background information. *The instructor should made it clear, while this information is being presented, that it will not be included in any evaluation.*

The test should be based on the learning objectives, and then the course material should be developed so that it includes everything in the test. This sequence ensures that the training remains focused on the necessary skills and values of the trainees. At the same time, the safety instructor should be alert to unplanned but nevertheless significant benefits that accrue from spontaneous discussions during training. "[Instructors] presently are making progress . . . of which we are perhaps dimly aware, . . . and that contribute[s] toward goals which are unrecognized . . . but which are often worthy."[1] If the training diverges into fruitful discussions, the instructor should note the content and include it in the appropriate section of the next training program.

One of the most important guidelines for evaluation is that it must match the domain of learning in which the subject was taught and in which the trainee will be performing out in the field. When this rule is violated in production, the result is often substandard quality products. When it is violated in safety training, the results can be serious injuries. There may be occasions when the evaluator is not the instructor, and it becomes evident to the evaluator that, because of a mismatch between the training content and the test, or the learning objectives and the test, the trainee is not being fairly evaluated with respect to the skills necessary to work safely on the job. The evaluator, in this case, is obligated to notify the training supervisor or other appropriate management personnel of the problem, and to ensure that the trainee is not placed at risk.

EVALUATION METHODS

Classroom (cognitive) skills may be tested by written or oral exams. There are various forms of test questions, each with its own benefits and limitations (see Table 8.1).

TABLE 8.1   Test Question Techniques

Format	Benefit	Limitations
Multiple choice	Easy to grade and statistically analyze No problem with evaluator subjectivity	Difficult to measure trainees' ability to recall unprompted information Difficult to determine trainees' ability to organize information or make creative responses
Short answer	Easy to grade Trainee not prompted by selection of answers	Slight problem with objectivity; not a creative format
Essay	Good for measuring organizational skills, ability to formulate and articulate an extended, unprompted response	Time consuming to grade; difficult to evaluate objectively
Matching	Easy to grade; no problem with objectivity Good for determining if trainee grasps basic relationships	Question prompts the answer; does not elicit extended responses
Completion	Easy to grade Requires trainee's unprompted recollection	Not suitable for measuring high-level cognitive skills Slight problems with objectivity

Hands-on skills must be tested by requiring the trainee to demonstrate the skills. Attitudes, however, are quite difficult to test. The instructor must decide what types of behaviors are demonstrated by people with the proper attitude and then observe if trainees demonstrate those same behaviors when they have other options available.

Evaluations should match the training: it would seem too obvious a rule to dwell on. Of course the test should be designed to measure the skills taught in the class. Of course the training should be presented so that it matches the skills taught on the job. Then why do evaluations frequently not match the training? The answer is *convenience*. The most convenient test to develop, administer, and check is the written test. The easiest written test to grade and statistically interpret is the multiple-choice written test. Thus multiple-choice tests are as common as bees at a picnic and just as likely to undermine the purpose of the affair. There is nothing inherently wrong with multiple-choice testing; as illustrated above, it has its applications. But like every test method, it also has its limitations. The problems with multiple-choice testing occur when instructors value the ease of correcting the tests over the appropriateness of the evaluation method.

Inappropriate testing can result in tragedy. In safety and health training, trainees are often being instructed in skills necessary to protect their own life (as with hazardous material spill cleanup) or to save someone else's life (as with cardiopulmonary resuscitation). Hazardous material spill cleanup has very high cognitive (mental knowledge) and psychomotor (hands-on skills) components. Unless one wears it, one cannot comprehend the extent to which the protective equipment required for the cleanup of an unknown spilled material—the whole-body suit and the self-contained breathing apparatus—hampers vision and dexterity and generates heat stress.

Trainees cannot properly don the protective equipment and adjust it for use by reading a description or even watching a live demonstration. These skills cannot be measured on a written test. An evaluation instrument must be developed that allows the instructor to observe the trainees perform. That instrument should have a description of the proper actions, common mistakes for which to observe, and standards of performance. Trainees must practice the skills to learn them, and must be tested in a manner that requires them to demonstrate the skills.

Evaluation can determine if knowledge and skills are being successfully conveyed to the trainees, but evaluation of training does not determine whether the trainees, once armed with their new knowledge and skills, will be safer and more competent workers. To determine safety training's impact on on-the-job performance and safety, training personnel must endeavor to determine if there is any causal relationship between training and safe behavior.

If trainees are evaluated by their supervisors on the basis of compliance with safety rules, then instructors can calculate the correlation between test scores during training and performance on the job. The results of such hard mathematical analysis will often be humbling, if not positively humiliating, to the training and safety personnel who have developed and presented safety training programs, because it is often difficult to establish a positive correlation between on-the-job performance and training.

This was the experience of an instructor who attempted to establish a correlation between test performance and on-the-job performance for quality-control technicians. He asked the technicians to select a battery of tests that they believed to be related to their performance on the job. The instructor then administered the tests and correlated the test scores to peer and supervisor performance evaluations of the same quality-control inspectors. There was no significant positive correlation between any test, or combination of tests, and the performance evaluations. There were, however, significant negative correlations between the ages of the quality-control inspectors and their performance on tests. Apparently, the longer the quality-control inspectors had been away from academic environments, the more poorly they did on the tests. But some of these older, more experienced workers received the highest performance ratings.

The tests, although identified by the people performing the work as measuring on-the-job performance, did not reliably measure anything except time away from school. If statistical comparison of test performance to on-the-job performance had not been undertaken, these tests may have been unfairly used to evaluate and select personnel. This mistake was avoided because statistical analysis was utilized to measure the appropriateness of a test. But more important, the statistical analysis was performed because the role of evaluation was not limited to testing the trainees; it included evaluation of the program elements, including testing.

CHAPTER EIGHT REVIEW AND APPLICATION

1. List the components of a safety training program that are subject to evaluation.

2. List two methods of reducing the amount of anxiety trainees experience when they take a test.

3. To ensure fair evaluation, to what should the test questions be matched?
   a. The learning objectives
   b. The lecture content
   c. The job hazard analysis
   d. The cost-benefit analysis

Employees are being trained in hazardous spill response. The training is limited to safely identifying the hazard using various types of documentation (Material Safety Data Sheets, labels, and so on) and instrumentation (sensor tubes, explosive gas meters, and so on).
   What training content, if any, would be in the:

4. Affective domain?

5. Cognitive domain?

6. Psychomotor domain?

7. List two factors, other than performance on the evaluation, that would determine competency for employees assigned to carry out initial hazardous spill response in the workplace (as opposed to in the classroom).

8. What type of evaluation is easiest to analyze statistically?
   a. Short answer
   b. Essay question
   c. Multiple choice
   d. Hands-on demonstration

9. Give an example of information that might be presented in class but would not be incorporated into the trainee's evaluation.

10. When should the test questions be drafted? Write one sentence justifying your answer.
   a. Before the training content is developed
   b. After the training content is developed
   c. Before determining training needs
   d. After determining training needs

REFERENCES

1. J. Myron Atkin, "Behavioral Objectives in Curriculum Design: A Cautionary Note," *The Science Teacher* 35, no. 5 (May 1968): 234.

2. Walter Dick and Lou Carey, *The Systematic Design of Instruction* (Glenview, IL: Scott Foresman and Company, 1978), 83.

IMPROVING THE PROGRAM

KEY CONCEPT OF CHAPTER NINE

*S*afety training program improvement should address all elements of the course development process, the presentation, and the evaluation techniques.

Evaluation is not limited to training; it is a common behavior and a part of many everyday activities. For example, it would be possible to create games so that no competition was involved, but games like that would never become popular. People like to know how they are doing, and they cannot know unless they can compare their performance with some objective measure. In the case of games, that measure is how their current performance compares with some other performance. The other performance may be that of an opposing player or team, or one's own performance during past attempts at the game.

On-the-job behavior is, in this respect, no different from recreational behavior. People usually want feedback on their performance; trainees want to know if they are meeting the expectations of their instructors, and instructors want to know if they are successful in inculcating the skills, knowledge, and values necessary for the trainees to perform their work safely. Most instructors want to be fair and objective in evaluating their trainees, and they hope their instructional skills will be judged by the same criteria.

Therein lies a problem. While evaluation is an absolutely critical component of program improvement, and most individuals involved in the processes of delivering and developing training wish to receive feedback on their performance, the personnel who carry out the evaluation are still likely to encounter some resistance. Just as trainees often suffer from anxiety at the prospect of being tested, company training personnel suffer anxiety at the prospect of being evaluated. Consequently, the evaluators should expect some problems to occur. It will be difficult for them to anticipate in what form this resistance to evaluation will manifest itself, but they should be forewarned it will happen, and should not be surprised or discouraged when the evaluation does not proceed smoothly. There are a couple of approaches the evaluators can take that may help minimize this resistance. First, they can work hard to assure the training personnel being evaluated that the standards being used are fair—possibly by including those personnel in the development of the evaluation instrument. Second, they can design the instrument so that those who are evaluated have an opportunity to present a written response to any rating that they believe is unfair.

Once an evaluation is completed and deficiencies are identified, corrective actions must be formulated and implemented. The implementation may be a major project in itself, but it will probably receive strong corporate support. Generally, once the painful process of clearly identifying deficiencies is completed, and training personnel are in agreement as to what those deficiencies are, the implementation of corrective actions will proceed smoothly.

The ultimate measure of any company's safety training program is the role the program plays in protecting employees from injuries, which itself is a broader reflection of the company's dedication to quality. "Industry leaders come to attention when mishaps are expressed in quality of decision-making and industrial excellence—not simply a task of keeping employees out of the hospital."[1]

EVALUATION STRATEGIES

Educators have identified two processes and two products that are involved in educational evaluation (see Table 9.1). To ensure quality training—training that changes the behavior of the trainees so that they perform work in a fashion that minimizes the possibility of their becoming sick or injured—all four components must be evaluated. Then the training program must be revised based on the results of the evaluation. This two-step process—identifying training program deficiencies through evaluation, and implementing corrections of those deficiencies—constitutes program improvement.

We will consider each of the processes and products that must be evaluated.

PROGRAM DEVELOPMENT

The training program development process itself should be subject to evaluation. The most important area of this evaluation has to do with the match between learning needs and training content.

TABLE 9.1   Evaluation Matrix

Processes	Products
Program development	The training program
Presentation of training	The trainee

The evaluation instrument should determine that all hazards have been identified and studied, and that the topics covered in training match the training needs identified in the job hazard analysis. If these steps have not been carried out, it is likely that employees are being inappropriately trained. The training may be inappropriate in that behavior changes are being promoted to deal with safety hazards that should have been eliminated through engineering or administrative controls, or it may be that important safety training topics are being missed altogether.

The steps that were initially used to develop the training can be modified into a checklist form to evaluate the quality of the development process. A sample checklist is below.

- Has every task performed at the facility been subjected to a job hazard analysis (JHA)? (List all occupations here and check with the company's human resources department to ensure that the list is complete.) Write the date of the job hazard analysis next to each (see Table 9.2 for an example).

- Is there a written program in place for updating the JHA whenever equipment or procedures change? (*Comment:* This can be checked by reviewing records of engineering modifications and checking them against records of JHA updates.)

- Is there a program for tracking recommendations made by the JHA committee until they are implemented? (*Comment:* Written records should be available stating whether each recommendation was accepted or rejected and how it was implemented.)

- Have all recommendations for safety training been rewritten as behavioral objectives? (*Comment:* There should be a direct relationship between the recommendations of the JHA committee and the training objectives. This relationship is not necessarily one for one. A single objective may cover several of the JHA committee's train-

TABLE 9.2   Documentation of JHA Surveys

Occupation	Date of JHA	Date of Next JHA
Mechanic	4-22-87	
Millwright	2-5-88	
Word processor	3-17-89	

TABLE 9.3   Training Program Objectives Derived from JHA Committee Recommendations

Example 1

Several training objectives derived from one JHA committee recommendation.

JHA T1 (job hazard analysis recommendation—training, number 1): Plant operators need training in cleaning up spilled hydrazine.

OT1A (objective derived from recommendation T1, first): Describe, without prompting, the proper respiratory protection for hydrazine.

OT1B: State the proper persons to notify when detecting a chemical spill.

OT1C: List all the health and safety hazards associated with hydrazine.

Example 2

Several JHA committee recommendations that are covered by one objective.

JHA T2: Forklift drivers should check the vehicle's brakes before driving.

JHA T3: Forklift drivers should ensure that warning light, horn, and backup alarm are operational before driving.

OT2: The trainee shall be able to perform a complete safety check on a forklift within three minutes, with 100 percent accuracy.

ing recommendations, or several objectives may be necessary to cover one objective. If the original recommendations were coded, it is much easier to check them against the objectives.) (Table 9.3.)

- Were engineering or administrative controls first considered prior to recommending training as the corrective action for a hazard?

☐ THE TRAINING PROGRAM

- Are all the desired behaviors for the program expressed as behavioral objectives?

- Are all the desired behaviors confirmed with the appropriate type of evaluation (written or oral tests for cognitive skills, hands-on demonstrations for psychomotor skills)?

- Have the workers for whom the training is intended and the subject matter experts had an opportunity to review the training and make recommendations?

- Are key topics conveyed by at least two types of media?

- Are the necessary audiovisual aids (VCR, monitor, overhead projector), support services (duplicating, typing), and facilities (classroom or hands-on) available? (*Comment:* If not, do not assume the training cannot be presented. Take a hard look at every alternative method for presenting the training using available equipment and facilities.)

- Have the learning behaviors of the target population been taken into account?

- Have the objectives been tied to meaningful values?

- Is the pace of instruction set briskly enough to prevent boredom, but slow enough to ensure that the learners can comprehend the instruction?

- If one of the teaching techniques planned is moving from the known to the unknown, will a pretest be used to establish entry knowledge or skills?

- Do the training materials include anonymous evaluation forms that give the trainees the opportunity to evaluate both the course material and the instructors?

- Are remedial materials available for trainees who need them, and are enrichment materials available for advanced trainees?

☐ PRESENTATION OF TRAINING

- Are the instructors dressed in a manner that is not distracting to the trainees?

- Are the instructors knowledgeable enough about the material being taught to answer most questions immediately and to research the rest promptly?

- Are the training facilities appropriate (comfortable, seating free from distraction, audiovisual equipment in good working order, proper temperature)?

- Does the instructor encourage and clearly answer questions and in other ways display respect for the trainees?

- Was the lecture well organized, beginning with the learning objectives, developing key points systematically, and ending with a summary?

- Were all tests, hands-on or written, graded promptly, with the trainees given clear explanations as to why answers were correct or incorrect?

A note on the answer format: the trainees should be given an opportunity to answer these questions. They are the best qualified to do so. For many of these questions, some format other than (yes, no) will encourage the evaluator to make comments that will be useful in revising the training program or helping instructors to change their presentation techniques.

Numerical scales (sometimes referred to as *Likert scales*) are a popular format for marking responses to evaluations. Often numbers are listed from one through five, where the numbers above three are defined as indicating progressively stronger agreement and the numbers below three are defined as indicating progressively greater disagreement. The benefit of this format is that the trainees can express degrees of feeling about the course, and the resulting scales are particularly amenable to statistical analysis. One liability of any numerical scale is that, unless used with other evaluation techniques, it does not encourage constructive criticism (that is, criticism that includes creative solutions to the problems identified).

A technique that encourages the identification of specific strengths and weaknesses is to simply provide a few lines under each question and ask for a written answer. This can be used to generate recommendations for improvement if the evaluator is asked for such. The liability of this approach is that it does not allow for statistical analysis, or even summarizing. If the trainer is dealing with a large group of trainees, he or she may not have the time to review a large group of written answers and may prefer a summary of numerical ratings.

The first step in evaluation is reviewing the program development process. An important discovery may come out of that review—a finding that the job hazard analysis is incomplete. It is common, when making a first attempt at a job hazard analysis, to either miss reviewing some jobs that include potentially hazardous activities, or, if all jobs are included in the JHA, to miss some component tasks. Those jobs should be immediately subjected to the JHA process. Even before that takes place, though, the workers and supervisors responsible for that job should be queried to determine if they believe the hazards of their work could be reduced by additional safety training. Although the systematic JHA survey will undoubtedly identify more hazards and training needs, it will also take much more time, and there may be some obvious deficiency that can be immediately addressed.

The best way to ensure that the JHA remains current is not to wait for program evaluation, but to make JHA an ongoing process. If the safety department allots some time for JHA on a quarterly basis, it is unlikely that new equipment or procedures will ever be overlooked.

Those initial recommendations from the informal survey, and the ones that are generated from the JHA, should be incorporated into the lesson plans. This means objectives should be written to cover the skills identified, and then the instructional program (lesson plans, audiovisuals, practice sessions, texts, and so on) should be modified to give trainees the opportunity to learn and demonstrate the skills described in the objective.

Just as subject matter experts on the information provided by the safety training were queried as to what changes were to be made in a program, the same experts can be used to determine how those changes may be implemented. If company structure permits, those experts may actually work with the instructors in revising instructional materials.

Safety training goals should be continuously reviewed to determine whether engineering or administrative controls can be used to eliminate hazards, so that there is no longer any need for the training. *The finest training program is less preferable to obviating the need for the training by elimination of the hazard.*

1. (Complete this sentence) Evaluation is the act of determining if the object being evaluated meets _____ .

2. List two training program processes that are subject to evaluation.

3. List two training program products that are subject to evaluation.

4. All desired behavior outcomes of the training program should be described as:
   a. *Test questions*
   b. *Learning objectives*
   c. *Performance goals*
   d. *Identified needs*

5. Prior to initiating a systematic job hazard analysis, workers should be:
   a. *Queried as to any safety hazards that should be addressed immediately*
   b. *Interviewed to determine their learning characteristics*
   c. *Informed of the learning objectives of all safety and health training programs*
   d. *Given thorough pre-JHA physicals*

6. List two techniques that may help training department personnel overcome resistance to evaluation.

7. Write a job hazard analysis recommendation that might be generated at your place of employment.

8. Write at least two learning objectives that could be derived from the recommendation written in number 7.

Write one item that could be included in an evaluation of a:

9. Training presentation

10. Training development process

11. Training program

12. Trainee's performance

■ REFERENCES

1. William C. Pope, letter to the editor, *Occupational Hazards* (December 1991):10.

JUSTIFYING THE COST OF SAFETY TRAINING PROGRAMS

KEY CONCEPTS OF CHAPTER TEN

Success in implementing safety training programs, as well as success in advancing one's career, requires understanding the language and concepts of cost justification.

The costs of safety and health programs are far lower than the costs of not having these programs. Effective safety training usually results in net savings to the organization.

Most company executives do not understand the actual costs of industrial accidents. Determining these costs is a critical step in justifying safety training expenses.

What is an arm worth? Or eyesight? Or mobility? Or freedom from pain? Or the absence of disfigurement? All of these things and many others—including life itself—are assigned worth in the worker's compensation manual. But most of us think of such items as simply priceless, and we rebel against the thought of putting a price on worker health. This book is based on the principle that the health and life of our co-workers are simply priceless.

That does not, however, absolve safety program developers and instructors from the responsibility of understanding and applying the principles of cost-benefit analysis to their work. On the contrary, *the promotion of occupational safety requires the ability to understand and perform cost-benefit analysis.* The health of workers may be priceless, but the value of safety training, until justified, is simply an add-on expense. It is one component in the entire safety process, which in turn is one component of the cost of doing business. Determining the slice that training receives of the safety budget pie requires establishing, in terms of costs and benefits, exactly how much it will contribute to company safety goals.

Business and industry, and the salary and benefits they provide, are major contributors to maintaining the health of Americans. There has been ample documentation that both the physical and mental health of many people decline when they lose their jobs. The health of entire communities suffers when companies that provide jobs are shut down. No matter what the underlying sympathies of safety personnel, whether for management or labor, they should realize that everyone benefits when safety training programs, like other company functions, are designed with an eye toward the net costs and the resulting benefits. To assess the value of both costs and benefits, measurable standards must be developed for both. According to one chemical plant safety officer, "You can't control what you can't measure." His interviewer writes, "It is important to measure actual and potential costs of such items as Workers' Compensation, property losses, and pollution liabilities, conduct risk analysis, and then establish priorities for controls and programs."[1] That statement was made about safety in general, but it applies equally to each component of which the safety program is composed, including safety training.

There is a pervasive quality about the cost-benefit perspective. The concept of "cost" goes beyond the concept of profit, or even that of money. People want to see the maximum results for the effort they exert. This is a universal human trait. It is a trait that is highly developed in the business world. It provides safety instructors with a powerful tool for persuading decision makers as to the value of safety training. The potential for cost reduction is staggering: on a national level, occupational injuries and illnesses cost the United States $83 billion per year. "The effect of all this on the economy? An $83 billion price tag for medical and lost work time costs, according to the Rand Institute."[2]

Justifying the cost of safety training is not normally considered part of the program development process. It is an administrative, not a developmental, concern. It is included here because this book is directed toward private, as opposed to academic, institutions. In the private sector, understanding the principles of cost-benefit analysis is as essential to success in any endeavor as a competence in one's job responsibilities. First-line supervisors, middle managers, and executives—all the way up to chief executive officers—think and speak in terms of cost versus benefit.

The ability to address the affective domain—to convince people of the need to change unsafe equipment, work practices, and behaviors—is a necessary part of the overall competency of all safety personnel. Safety personnel are "missionaries" for safety. If safety instructors cannot speak the language of the natives, they cannot change the natives' beliefs. And in the business world, the language of the natives is definitely cost versus benefit. Every program that is recommended, every piece of equipment of more than nominal cost, is going to be considered from this perspective. If it is not, find a new employer—this one will not long remain in business.

Safety, and consequently safety training, which is a necessary component of the safety program, can be justified on a cost-benefit basis. Consider the experience of Will Burt, an Ohio steel fabricating firm: "In 1990, worker's compensation costs were one-tenth what they were five years ago. Health insurance costs rose less than 1.5 percent during the same period, while increasing more than 83 percent elsewhere."[3] Consider also this statistic from Control Data Corporation: "The typical 40-year-old man who doesn't wear a seat belt, smokes two packs of cigarettes a day, and is 30% overweight costs his employer $1282 a year in medical bills, double the $631 spent on someone the same age with healthier habits."[4] Safe behaviors on or off the job translate into lower business expenses. Conversely, unsafe behaviors—on or off the job—cost the employer, often dearly.

But is it ethical even to think in terms of cost when considering safety programs? Yes, it is, for several reasons. First, in most cases, adults and their dependents are healthier when the adults are gainfully employed, particularly if the employer provides medical benefits. Safety hazards that make the employees' work unprofitable may eventually cause loss of the job. The employees' health and safety would probably decline at this point.

All activity involves risk. The goal of an occupational safety program is to minimize the total risk of the job, not just one of the job's tasks. The highest risk activity that the average American engages in is driving, which claims 50,000 American lives per year and another quarter million injuries. We could eliminate all of those injuries by making driving illegal. Why then don't we do so? The answer is that the consequences would be disastrous to the health of American workers. Millions of good jobs would be lost in the automobile and related industries. Additional millions would be lost because people would be unable to commute to their jobs. Communities hit by unemployment have much higher illness and mortality rates. So in every respect, eliminating automobiles would be a very bad way of reducing driving deaths. The same can be said of safety solutions that would drive the employer out of business. They would cause much more harm to the worker than good, unless it has been determined that it is absolutely impossible to determine a safe way of performing the work. For example, the manufacturing of asbestos-containing insulation has been eliminated in this country. In this case, where the risk is so high and so difficult to control, the workers are indeed better off unemployed then employed in an industry that puts them at high risk of contracting asbestosis, lung cancer, or mesothelioma.

If management is committed to safety, they are going to want the most "bang for the buck," that is, the most reduction in risk for the money spent. If management is not committed to safety, it is because they do not see it as contributing to the bottom line. They see it as an expense that must be minimized. In this case the safety instructors need to convince management that the safety department or the training department (whichever they work for) can be viewed as a "profit center," and that the process of training is critical to company survival. "Employee training, once a minor concern . . . must move toward center stage. [I]nadequate training costs firms and workers—in downtime, defective parts or equipment, wasted material, health and safety risks, late deliveries, and poor customer service."[5] Consider that list: *downtime, defective parts or equipment, wasted material, health and safety risks, late deliveries, poor customer service.* All of those are indisputably profit/loss concerns. All are exacerbated by inadequate safety training, and very likely their impact is underestimated. According to certified safety professional William Allison, "Conventional loss costs are extremely misleading. While injury costs may be a relatively minor item in some businesses, total costs may be as high as over 90 times injury costs. For example, an oil company found that its actual loss costs of over $5.7 million compared to injury costs of only $60,500. Manufacturers often find loss costs total about 10 times workmen's compensation costs."[6]

Is the safety department a profit center for the company? You bet. And safety training is a major contributor. Safety is one area where sometimes minor changes in policy, costing little or nothing, can result in substantial, measurable savings.

PERFORMING A COST-BENEFIT STUDY

In one sense, performing a cost-benefit study (see, for example, Table 10.1) is like developing a training program: start with a goal and work backward. Personnel undertaking a cost-benefit justification should select something that they believe will result in a meaningful improvement in the safety and health of the workers at their facility. This can be the purchase of a single piece of equipment, a change in policy that may either add labor time to an existing procedure or create a new procedure, or a policy change that will make existing purchases more expensive (for example, getting approval for upgraded coveralls that are fireproof).

TABLE 10.1 Cost Analysis

Expenses involved in presenting training	
Tuition for 50 employees at $45.00 each	$2,750
Four hours lost work time each at $15.00/hour	3,000
Four hours replacement work time each at $15.00/hour	3,000
Total expenses	8,750
Total savings with expenses taken into account	141,560
	8,750
	$132,810

In this case, the cost-benefit will focus on safety training. Let's say that a company already meets minimum OSHA requirements for providing first aid on the job; they have first aid kits up, a contract for emergency transport with an ambulance firm, and at least one person per shift trained in first aid. Safety personnel believe that having about 25 percent of the work force also trained in CPR would increase the likelihood that victims of a breathing or cardiac emergency would receive aid within two or three minutes of the emergency occurring.

This is a difficult type of training on which to perform a cost analysis. Unlike many types of safety training, CPR does not address a common accident in business settings. If it did, the trainer could identify the savings of worker's compensation, other insurance, and lost work time as costs saved by having employees available who are trained in CPR. But "difficult" does not mean "impossible." Even this type of training can be subjected to analysis.

First, write a goal: establish that it is in the company's interest to provide CPR training to at least 25 percent of its employees. A person writing a cost-benefit analysis must keep in mind that, after performing the analysis, the numbers may indicate that the original idea is not cost-effective. It is important to try to remain objective and open to the possibility that one's original flash of inspiration may dim under the exposure of a systematic analysis.

Now write all the benefits of accomplishing that goal. Consider how it will benefit the company as whole, the employees who receive the training, and the employees who may need the skills of the trainees. The following list presents possible benefits:

- Employee morale will improve because they are being provided with an additional benefit—one that could be used at home as well as at work.

- Training records will look good to outsiders who are interested in a company's efforts to protect its employees or minimize loss (insurance loss-control agents, OSHA compliance officers, and so on).

- Possibly one employee every three years will receive prompt emergency rescue from a heart attack or choking emergency who would otherwise not have received it soon enough.

- Perhaps one employee family member per year will receive emergency rescue from a trained employee.

- CPR training includes a review of risk factors for cardiac emergencies. Perhaps two trainees per year will be persuaded to reduce a controllable risk factor (for example, lose weight, exercise, quit smoking, go on a stress-reduction program).

Assign dollar values to each benefit, including those that might be considered intangible, such as improvement in morale. List a cost saving for each benefit. Do not hesitate to be speculative in assigning cost savings. Every cost estimate, no matter how complex or systematic, includes some speculation. None of us are clairvoyant, and a cost analysis, whether justifying a CPR program or the building of a new mall, always represents some person's or some group's best guess. Include a rationale for each cost saving.

The following samples include some "soft" benefits (e.g., morale of the work force and appearance of training records) that are not particularly amenable to cost analysis, and some "hard" benefits (e.g., projected decreases in accident severity) that can be easily related to dollar savings. While most decision-makers will probably find the latter group of benefits more persuasive, all the benefits listed are "real life"; they express observable and meaningful, albeit sometimes difficult to measure, changes in the occupational environment. The cost-benefit analysis would be a less-accurate predictor of consequences of change if the soft benefits were not included.

☐ BENEFIT

Employee morale will improve because they are being provided with an additional benefit—one that could be used at home as well as at work.

☐ SAVINGS

Improved morale may be expressed as improved attendance or better productivity, assuming that providing CPR classes alone results in a 5 percent improvement in attendance. The firm has 200 people. Last year they averaged three days off each, or 600 days off total. A 5 percent improvement would result in a savings of three employee days at an average cost of $120 per day, or $360. While the benefits of good morale are significant, they are difficult to predict or measure. This estimate is probably conservative.

☐ BENEFIT

Training records will look good to outsiders who are interested in a company's efforts to protect its employees or minimize loss (insurance loss-control agents, OSHA compliance officers, and so on).

☐ SAVINGS

Let's assume that this is good public relations for the firm. Let's further assume that providing the classes does as much good as a public relations representative could accomplish in two weeks. Two weeks' pay for a public relations representative, with benefits, is $900.

☐ BENEFIT

Possibly one employee every three years will receive prompt emergency rescue from a heart attack or choking emergency who would otherwise not have received it soon enough.

☐ SAVINGS

One employee every three years is saved from death or brain damage, or the extent of their injury is significantly reduced because of prompt administration of CPR by a co-worker. Let us conservatively estimate that the cost in life insurance and other payments and replacement costs if the employee dies, or medical care and other costs if the employee lives, is $200,000. The amount of annual savings is $70,000.

☐ BENEFIT

CPR training includes a review of risk factors for cardiac emergencies. Perhaps two trainees per year will be persuaded to reduce a controllable risk factor (for example, lose weight, exercise, quit smoking, go on a stress-reduction program).

☐ SAVINGS

One employee every three years is saved from death or brain damage. Let us conservatively estimate that the cost in life insurance and other payments and replacement costs if the employee dies, or medical care and other costs if the employee lives, is $200,000. The amount of annual savings is $70,000. Also, lost time due to illness is reduced an additional 5 percent. The amount saved is $360. The total annual savings without training costs taken into account equal $141,560.

An important factor in establishing costs and benefits in this type of safety training is that, if the company provides medical benefits, it ultimately pays for any health problems that the employees suffer, not just those that are the result of occupational injury. "The reality, from a loss control standpoint, however, is that whether an employee's wrist pain is actually carpal tunnel syndrome or is a work-related compensation claim, or an effect of hormonal or diabetic conditions covered by the group medical coverage, it is still contributing to the economic loss of the organization and the physical loss of the employee."[7]

It is critical that the safety training personnel understand this, and that they convince management of the reality of it, because worker's compensation costs are a very small portion of the true costs of injury or illness to a company. If a safety cost-benefit analysis is performed based only on worker's compensation costs, bad decisions will be made. Costs of injuries and illnesses include reduced productivity, training and salaries of replacement workers, and medical insurance. Any or all of these may be substantial expenses, and none of them is related to whether the injury or illness was occupational. If the injury is occupational, the employer has the additional expenses of worker's compensation, possible lawsuits, increased insurance, decreased morale of co-workers who now perceive the workplace to be a hazardous environment, and investigations into the injury.

One of the knottiest questions with which administrators of safety training deal is whether to use employees or vendors to deliver training. This is a good example of the type of question that can only be answered well after a cost-benefit analysis has been performed. Choosing between vendors and employees is not easy, and every case must be decided individually. Two things must be considered: whether vendors or employees can deliver the training at lower cost, and which of the groups will deliver the higher quality training.

One company, after analyzing both cost and quality, switched the delivery of two of their programs. First aid/CPR training had previously been taught by employees. Administrators looked at the total cost of the program, including the salary and benefits of the employees who taught the program, and the time employees devoted to acquiring and maintaining their first aid/CPR instructor certification with a nationally recognized certifying agency. Acquiring certification, in particular, was a significant expense because the company turned over instructors at a fairly high rate. There was also a noncost problem with providing the training in-house: instructors complained that they were under undue pressure to pass employees in these programs when their performance was marginal. The employees they were training were friends and co-workers, and passing CPR or first aid training was a requirement for some promotions.

Both factors, cost and quality, favored the use of vendors. Vendor charges for the training were lower than employee cost for teaching the programs in-house. And vendors, free from the social pressures generated by working with the personnel they evaluated, could make objective decisions regarding whether trainees successfully demonstrated the necessary skills. Since the company-specific content of first aid and CPR training was minimal (the training included only a brief review of company first aid response policy), there was no need to utilize experienced employees as teachers.

However, the same company came to an opposite conclusion with a different training program. They used vendors to introduce new training department personnel to instructional techniques and development. Either the personnel were sent to a university for the training, or university instructors were paid to teach the program at the company. Training administrators wanted the course to include a great deal of company-specific policies and procedures. In this case it proved to be more cost-effective to use experienced, in-house instructors to develop and deliver an instructor orientation program. The experience of the employees, not the up-front cost of the training, was the critical factor.

Sometimes it is difficult for administrators to quantify the value of experience. One corporation that had used an in-house construction crew for many years decided to contract out all construction work. Even though the per-hour costs of outside help were lower than those of employees, the total cost of construction proved to be higher because of the unfamiliarity of the vendor with the company's codes and standards.

In summary, dear safety training instructor, "The force is with you"—the costs are on your side. A training department that provides effective safety and health training is a profit center. The safety instructor who systematically identifies unsafe behaviors and then changes them has the same opportunities to improve his or her company's profitability as the most brilliant and innovative engineer or financial wizard. "Today we have a better opportunity to sell (safety) than at any time since the Industrial Revolution. . . . Injury and illness costs are higher than they've ever been. The regulatory emphasis on fines and penalties is greater than it's ever been. Liability problems and the penalties from criminal prosecutions are greater than they've ever been before."[8]

This is the age of industrial safety and health in developed countries. We have the challenge to prove that we can operate as efficiently as those countries where worker health and safety is not emphasized as highly. "Those countries," by the way, does not mean Japan. Occupational safety in Japan, even when differences in recording practices are taken into account, is at a higher level than it is in the United States. The law is with you, the costs are with you, your insurance company is with you, the union is with you, and enlightened management that understands the true costs of doing business is with you. You are doing the ethical thing.

Go out there and perform a cost-benefit analysis of a safety training program. Experienced safety and training personnel know they are preventing injuries and saving lives. They can prove they are saving money as well.

1. The Rand Institute estimates that occupational injuries cost the United States approximately _____ billion dollars per year.
   a. 10
   b. 19
   c. 47
   d. 83

2. For which of the following health problems does your company pay? (Circle all correct answers.)
   a. Occupational injuries
   b. Injuries that occur at home
   c. Illnesses caused by an unhealthy life-style
   d. Genetically induced illnesses

3. List at least three separate losses that may be incurred when an accident occurs on the job.

4. Write one safety training proposal for your company.

5. Write two benefits for the proposal written in question 4.

6. Assign a cost savings to the benefits described in question 5. For each, write one or two sentences providing a rationale for the savings.

7. Write two *values* to which you can appeal that would make a cost-benefit study supporting the proposal in question 4 more appealing.

8. A study of occupational safety in Japan indicated that the country's recent safety record is [better than, about the same as, worse than] (circle one) the record in the United States.

REFERENCES

1. Stephen Minter, "Quality and Safety: Unocal's Winning Combination," *Occupational Hazards* (October 1991):47.

2. Matthew P. Weinstock, "OSHA Reform: The Push for Worker Involvement," *Occupational Hazards* (December 1991):37.

3. Greg LaBar, "Worker Training: An Investment in Safety," *Occupational Hazards* (August 1991).

4. Robert Gottschall, "Safety Management and Total Employee Health Costs," *Professional Safety* 35, no. 7 (July 1990):27. Published by the American Society of Safety Engineers (ASSE), Desplaines, IL.

5. Congressional Office of Technology Assessment, "Worker Training: Competing in the New International Economy," quoted in Greg LaBar, "Urgent! Training Must Be Improved," *Occupational Hazards* (August 1991):24.

6. William W. Allison, "Are We Doing Enough?" *Professional Safety* 36, no. 2 (February 1991):31. Published by the American Society of Safety Engineers (ASSE), Desplaines, IL.

7. Robert Gottschall, "Safety Management and Total Employee Health Costs," p. 24.

8. Ray Bolston, quoted in Stephen G. Minter, "Creating the Safety Culture," *Occupational Hazards* 53, no. 8 (August 1991):19.

Acquired immune deficiency syndrome: An immune system disease.

Affective: Related to personal values.

AIDS: Acquired immune deficiency syndrome.

Cardiopulmonary resuscitation: A technique for assisting victims of breathing and circulation emergencies.

Carpal tunnel syndrome: A wrist and hand disorder often caused by repetitive-motion injuries.

Ceiling limit: A level of exposure to a chemical that OSHA does not permit exposure to for any part of the workday.

Centers for Disease Control: An agency of the Department of Health and Human Services that tracks and attempts to minimize the spread of disease.

Cognitive: Related to reasoning and calculation.

Condition: The part of a performance objective that specifies the situation in which the performance takes place.

Cost-benefit analysis: A comparison of the expenses and the advantages of a course of action.

CPR: Cardiopulmonary resuscitation.

Engineering controls: Improvements in equipment design that benefit worker safety.

Environmental Protection Agency: A government agency responsible for regulating environmental pollutants.

EPA: Environmental Protection Agency.

Ergonomics: The study of the physical interaction between workers and their environment.

Goal: A specific act that is to be accomplished.

IDLH: Immediately dangerous to life and health.

Immediately dangerous to life and health (IDLH): A level of chemical exposure that poses an immediate, serious health risk.

Industrial hygiene: The discipline of preventing occupationally related illnesses.

Instructional media: Any means used to communicate information during training.

JHA: Job hazard analysis.

Job hazard analysis: The review of job responsibilities with the intent of identifying and mitigating potential hazards.

Job rotation: The practice of reducing job hazards by setting limits on how long one worker may engage in a given activity.

Material Safety Data Sheet: A document that provides information about the health hazards of materials used on the job.

MSDS: Material Safety Data Sheet.

Objective: A precise statement of what a trainee will be able to accomplish as a result of learning.

Occupational Safety and Health Act: A body of law enforced by the Occupational Safety and Health Administration.

Occupational Safety and Health Administration: A government agency that regulates occupational activities that pose hazards to workers.

OSHA: 1. Occupational Safety and Health Act. 2. Occupational Safety and Health Administration.

PEL: Permissible exposure limit.

Performance: The part of a performance objective that specifies the action to take place.

Permissible exposure limit: Amount of a chemical, averaged over eight hours, above which OSHA does not permit a worker to be exposed.

Personal protective equipment (PPE): Equipment, such as hard hats and respirators, designed to protect workers from occupational injuries.

Psychomotor: Related to body-mind coordination.

Repetitive-motion injuries: Bodily injury caused by moving body parts through unnatural ranges of motion.

Risk: The degree of possibility that an activity may have an undesirable outcome.

Safety: The prevention of occupational accidents.

Standard: The portion of an objective that specifies the quality of the activity that takes place.

Total Quality Management: A philosophy and process for ensuring that occupational products and services best serve those people for whom they are intended.

TQM: Total Quality Management.

Work practices: Specific techniques for carrying out job responsibilities.

Worker's compensation: A government-mandated disability insurance program.

BIBLIOGRAPHY

Accident Prevention Manual for Industrial Operations, 7th ed. Chicago, IL: National Safety Council, 1978.

Continuing Learning in the Professions, Cyril O. Houle. San Francisco: Jossey-Bass, 1981.

Developing Vocational Instruction, R. Mager and K. Beach. Belmont, CA: Pitman Management and Training, 1967, Library of Congress #67–26846.

Educational Evaluation, Theory and Practice, B. L. Worthen and J. R. Sanders. Belmont, CA: Wadsworth, 1993.

Improving Managerial Effectiveness: A Handbook of Development Strategies, ed. L. W. Hellervik and B. L. Davis. Minneapolis, MN: Personnel Decisions, Inc., 1984.

Instructing for Results, F. H. Margolis and C. R. Bell. Minneapolis, MN: Lakewood Publications, 1986.

Measuring Instructional Intent, R. F. Mager. Belmont, CA: Fearon Pitman Publishers, Inc., 1973.

The Supervisor and On-the-Job Training, M. M. Broadwell. Reading, MA: Addison-Wesley, 1974.

The Systematic Design of Instruction, W. Dick and R. Cary. Glenview, IL: Scott Foresman and Company, 1978.

Taxonomy of Educational Objectives, Handbook I: Cognitive Domain, ed. Benjamin S. Bloom. New York: David McKay, Inc., 1956.

Taxonomy of Educational Objectives, Handbook II: Affective Domain, eds. David R. Krathwohl, Benjamin S. Bloom, and Bertram S. Masia. New York: David McKay, Inc., 1956.

Training and Development Handbook, 3rd ed., ed. R. L. Craig. New York: McGraw-Hill, 1987.

An italic *f* or *t* following a page number denotes that the entry is found in either a *figure* or *table* on the cited page.

Goggles, evaluation of, 9
Government safety regulations, 49–51. *See also* OSHA regulations
Group awards, 7
Guidelines
for conducting training, 103–117, 108*f*–111*f*
for presentations, 114–117
for sequencing of instruction, 97
Guide to Hazardous Chemicals (DOT), 72

Hands-on learning, 87, 94
Hard benefits, versus soft in cost-benefit analysis, 147–149
Hard hats, evaluation of, 9
Hazard(s)
common citations, 50*t*
communication of, 107–108
control of, 5
identifying, 20
nontraining approaches to, 53–57, 53*t*, 86
OSHA regulations and. *See* OSHA regulations
root causes, 21–22
See also Risk(s)
Hazard communication standard (OSHA regulation 29 CFS 1910.1200), 107
Hazardous exposure, 2
Health, of worker, 142–151
Health hazards, identifying, 20
Health insurance costs, 43, 143, 149
Hearing protection
evaluation of, 9
functions and limitations, 11
HIV (human immunodeficiency virus), 84

IDLH (Immediately dangerous to life and health), 112, 113
Illness
cost-benefit analysis and, 142–151
worker predisposition to, 2
See also Hazard(s)
Immediately dangerous to life and health (IDLH), 112, 113
Indicators, of safety training need, 41–44, 41*t*
Industrial workers, office workers versus, 4–5
In-house training, versus vendor-supplied, 87–89, 115, 150–151
Injury(ies)
cost-benefit analysis and, 142–151
prevention, 2
during training, 80
U.S. statistics for, 4
worker predisposition to, 2
Instruction, sequencing guidelines for, 97
Instructional materials, 26, 96
developing and selecting, 86–90, 91*f*
structuring, 78, 90–98
variety of, 86–87
Instructor. *See* Safety trainer(s)
Insurance rates, 43
Interests, of safety trainees, 81*t*, 84–85
Interview, of accident victims, 40
Investigation, as safety policy component, 120

Japan, occupational safety in, 151
JHA. *See* Job hazard analysis (JHA)

Job
  defined, 37
  hazard potential, 81
  job hazard analysis and, 39
  physical qualifications and,
    80–82
Job competency, 40
Job description
  accident trends and, 40
  draft review, 38
  safety training survey and, 39
  writing, 37
Job hazard analysis, 20, 23*f*
Job hazard analysis (JHA)
  conditions indicating need for,
    44–45
  fundamentals of, 36–41
  OSHA regulations and, 50–51
  training evaluation and,
    134–135, 134*t*, 135*t*,
    138
Job performance
  physical characteristics and,
    80–82, 81*t*
  training correlated with,
    122–127
Job rotation, 55

Knowledge, and job hazard analysis, 22–24

Laboratory standard (OSHA regulation 1910.1450), compliance with, 57–58
Leadership, of supervisor, 40
Learning
  defined, 102
  disequilibrium and, 114, 115
  domains, 59–61, 59*t*
Learning activities and materials
  developing and selecting,
    24–29, 86–90, 91*f*

structuring. *See* Structuring, of
    learning activities and ma-
    terials
Learning objectives
  benefit of conveying to trainee,
    115
  components of, 69–75, 69*t*
  defined, 66, 67
  review of, in training, 106
  writing of, 67–75
Lesson plan, writing, 90, 91*f*–92*f*
Likert scales, 137
Limitations
  for chemical exposure. *See*
    Chemicals, dose and rela-
    tive risk
  of respirators, 9–11, 10*f*
  of testing formats, 125–127,
    125*t*
Loss. *See* Cost-benefit analysis

Mager, R., 79, 80
Management
  role in training, 115
  worker attitude toward, 7
Manual, company procedure,
    37
Manufacturing errors, 43
Materials, instructional. *See* In-
    structional materials
Material Safety Data Sheets,
    103–104, 107, 108*f*–111*f*
  for chlorine, 112
Medical emergency-response pro-
    gram, 12
Medical insurance costs, 143,
    149
Mission statement, 18–19
  training goals and learning ob-
    jectives, 66
Mistakes, in manufacture and op-
    eration, 43

Morale, employee, 146
Motivation, of safety trainees,
    81*t*, 83–84
Motivational training, 56, 97

National Fire Protection Association, 95
National Institute of Occupational Health and Safety, 43
National Safety Council, *Accident Prevention Manual* publication, 40
Numerical scales, 137

Objectives
    learning. *See* Learning objectives
    training, evaluation and, 134–136, 135*t*
Observation, of workers, 38
Occupational Exposure to Hazardous Chemicals in Laboratories (OSHA regulation 1910.1450), 57–58
Occupational hazards. *See* Hazard(s)
Occupational risk. *See* Risk(s)
Occupational Safety and Health Act/Administration. *See* OSHA; OSHA regulations
Occupational safety program. *See* Safety program
Office workers, injuries among, 4–5
Operating errors, 43
Organization excellence, safety and, 3
Organizations. *See* Company(ies)
OSHA, 23*f*
    accident documentation requirements, 42

job hazard analysis publication, 20, 23*f*
    mandatory safety policy proposed by, 11
    training definitions, 29, 94, 102
OSHA regulations
    chemical exposure (regulation 20 CFS 1910.1000), 112
    compliance with, 49, 50–51, 57–58, 95–96, 107
    hazard communication standard (29 CFS 1910.1200), 107
    laboratory standard (1910.1450), 57–58
    Respiratory Protection (29 CFR 1910.134), 54
    training, 49
OSHA Requirements in OSHA Standards and Training Guides, 49–51
Overexposure, 107, 108*f*–111*f*

Part-time workers, defined, 2
PEL. *See* Permissible exposure limit (PEL)
Performance of trainee, stating as learning objective, 69
Permissible exposure limit (PEL), 112
Personalization, of training, 104
Personal protective equipment (PPE)
    hazard correction via, 56–57
    hearing protection, 11
    respirators, 9–11
    role in safety, 9–11
Physical characteristics, role in training and job performance, 80–82, 81*t*
Physical disabilities, in the workplace, 81

Physical injury. *See* Injury(ies)
Pilot program, 103–104
Powerlessness, of worker, 6–7
PPE. *See* Personal protective
   equipment (PPE)
Predisposition, to injury or ill-
   ness, 2
Presentation
   guidelines, 114–117
   outlines, 116–117
Prevention, of worker injuries,
   2
Problem-solving, safety training
   as method of, 51
Problem workers, 39
Process (work)
   evaluation and, 133–134, 138
   new, implementation of, 42
Products, of training, evaluating,
   133, 133*t*
Profit. *See* Cost-benefit analysis
Protection, of workers, 2. *See also*
   OSHA regulations
Protective equipment. *See* Personal protective equip-
   ment (PPE)
Psychomotor learning domain,
   59*t*, 60

Quality
   defining in learning objectives,
     73
   in-house versus vendor-
     supplied training, 150
   of training environment, 105
   of work environment, 4
   in the workplace, 72–73

Rand Institute, 143
Reaction, to chemicals, 109–113
Record keeping. *See* Documenta-
   tion

Red flags, indicating need for
   safety training, 41–44, 41*t*
Relative risk, of chemicals, 109–
   113
Reporting, as safety policy component, 12
Respirators
   evaluation of, 9
   functions and limitations, 9–11,
     10*f*
   for hazard reduction, 56
Respiratory Protection (OSHA
   regulation 29 CFR
   1910.134), 54
Risk(s)
   chemical. *See* Chemicals, dose
     and relative risk
   cost-benefit analysis and,
     144–145
   industrial versus office workers,
     4–5
   reduction of, 2, 5
   See also Hazard(s)
Root causes
   of behaviors, 22
   of hazards, 21–22

Safety
   in Japan, 151
   organizational excellence and, 3
Safety glasses, for hazard reduction, 56
Safety hazard(s). *See* Hazard(s)
Safety policy, 11–12
   benefit of, 12
   components, 12*t*
Safety program
   components/component syn-
     ergy, 3, 3*t*
   cost-effectiveness, 5–6
   effect on worker, 6
   need for, 2–4

Stress indicators, workers as, 39
Structuring, of learning activities
    and materials, 78, 90–98
  instruction sequencing, guide-
    lines, 97
  short program series, 95–96
  single program, 97–98
Success, of training, 102–103,
    104, 114–117
Supervisor, weak versus strong, 40
Surveys
  job hazard analysis, 134*t. See
    also* Job hazard analysis
    (JHA)
  on safety training, 39*t*
Synergism, of safety program
    components, 3

Task
  defined, 37
  job hazard analysis and, 39
Task analysis, 39
Testing, 25, 96, 98, 122–127
  fairness, 122–123
  inappropriate, results of, 126
  job performance and, 126–127
  learning objectives as basis of,
    123–124
  methods, 124–127, 125*t*
  program evaluation and, 137
  standards, 123
Tools, role in safety, 8–9
Total Quality Management
  (TQM), 4, 19
Trainee. *See* Safety trainee(s)
Trainer. *See* Safety trainer(s)
Training. *See* Safety training
Training goals, 66–67
Training program. *See* Safety
    training program

U.S. Bureau of Labor Statistics, 4

U.S. Centers for Disease Control,
    4

Values, of safety trainees
  affecting training, 85
  trainer knowledge of, 115
Variance, from OSHA standards,
    50
Vendor-supplied training
  versus in-house, 87–89, 115,
    150–151
  tailoring to company needs,
    89–90

Will Burt Company, 143
Work environment, 3
  chemical exposure in, 112–113
  considered in writing learning
    objectives, 70–72
  design, 5
  health and quality of, 4
Worker(s)
  administrative controls and, 55
  Americans with Disabilities Act
    and, 81
  attitude modification, 6–7
  behaviors, 5
  chemical exposure, 112–113
  full-time versus part-time, 2
  hazard warnings and, 107–108
  health
    cost-benefit analysis and,
      142–151
    marginal, 40
  injury to
    prevention and protection, 2
    U.S. statistics for, 4
  laboratory, OSHA standard reg-
    ulating, 57–58
  as monitors, 39
  morale improvement among,
    146

new to job, 41
physical characteristics affecting
    training and job perfor-
    mance, 80–82
problem, 39
safety program affecting, 6
skills, safety and, 8
tools, safety and, 8–9
trainer observing, 38
in work environment, 5
See also Safety trainee(s)

Workplace. *See* Work environ-
    ment
Work practices, 55
Work process
    evaluation and, 133–134, 138
    new, implementation of, 42
Written statements
    cost-benefit analysis goals,
        146
    learning objectives, 67–75, 69t
    training goals, 66–67